AF706583

[illegible]
PROFESSIONAL CORPORATION

BY ATTORNEY BRIAN D. LERNER

ATTORNEY DRAFTED IMMIGRATION PETITIONS

By

Brian D. Lerner
Attorney at Law

© Copyright 2020 by Immigration Law Offices of Brian D. Lerner, APC
All rights reserved.
1047104

All rights Reserved. The petition/application enclosed herein may be altered or reproduced in any way the reader deems fit to meet the special requirements of his or her situation. However, no part of this publication or the information regarding the Law Offices of Brian D. Lerner, APC may be submitted to any Immigration Agency or any other agency of the Government. Attorney Brian D. Lerner does not give authorization to use his name or office in any way when submitting the revised petition or application to the Government.

Disclaimer and Terms of Use:

Effort has been made to ensure that the information in this book is accurate and complete. However, the author and the publisher do not warrant that this particular petition will mirror or be exactly as your situation. There has not been any attorney-client agreement created by the purchase of this petition or application. No legal advice has occurred. The cases, regulations and/or statutes cited may change at any time without notice.

There are a multitude of different immigration petitions and applications. They are complex and full of requirements. Obviously it would be best to hire an immigration attorney to best prepare the petitions and applications. However, this can certainly cost thousands of dollars.

The next best option is to get a sample of the petition written by an experienced immigration attorney. The samples cost a fraction what would be charged by an immigration attorney. However, while the reader has to alter, amend and change the parts of the sample petition to reflect their actual situation, it is a fantastic roadmap for them to use. If the reader has purchased the entire petition or application, they will have real live samples of cover letters, forms, declarations, affidavits and the necessary exhibits to use. The samples come from real cases and the names of those clients have been redacted to protect the privacy of that person or corporation.

These are petitions and applications that have been drafted by an experienced immigration attorney with over 25 years of experience. Get the benefits of that experience without the costs.

Brian D. Lerner has been a licensed attorney since 1992 and started the Law Offices of Brian D. Lerner, APC. The law practice consists of Immigration and Nationality Law and everything involved with and regarding immigration which includes citizenship, investment visas, family and employment visas, removal and deportation hearings, appeals, waivers, adjustment, consulate processing and all types of immigration and citizenship matters. Thousands of families have been reunited and/or permitted to stay in the U.S. and/or return to the U.S. because of the successful work of Immigration Attorney Brian D. Lerner.

This law offices handles all types of immigration cases including family based and employment based. Immigration issues range from immigration court proceedings to trying to fix what paralegals may have done that was neither correct nor proper. Foreign nationals must have experience lawyers admitted to practice law.

The Law Offices of Brian D. Lerner, APC handles cases arising from business visas, work permits, Green Cards, non-immigrant visas, deportation, citizenship, appeals and all areas of immigration. The Law Offices of Brian D. Lerner, APC does EB-5 Investor Visas, H-1B Specialty Occupation, L-1 Intracompany Transferee, E-2 Treaty Investor, E-1 Treaty Trader, O-1 Extraordinary Ability among others. Regarding immigrant visas for the Green Card, the firm does PERM and advanced degree PERM, Family Petitions, and Extraordinary Alien Petitions. In addition to affirmative petitions, the Law Firm represents people in people in deportation and removal hearings, including political asylum, withholding of removal, and convention against torture cases.

Brian D. Lerner has been certified as an expert in Immigration & Nationality Law by the California State Bar, Board of Legal Specialization since 2000 and has been recertified three times. He now passes on his decades of experience by allowing the Reader, Law Schools, Professors and other Immigration Attorneys to purchase sample petitions on every facet of Immigration Law.

Table of Contents

About the EB-3 I-140 Employer Petition

Do you have a Masters degree in a specialized field and a United States based company who is willing to sponsor you? You may qualify for an EB-3 I-140 petition. First, you will need to go through the PERM system to obtain a Labor Certification. Then you need to have an employer who is willing to sponsor you through the I-140 as the second step toward receiving a green card. Once the I-140 is approved, you can either adjust status or consulate process to actually get the Green Card. The EB-3 is a way for highly educated individuals to ultimately obtain their Green Card through employment based petitions.

ATTORNEY COVER LETTER

STATE BAR OF CALIFORNIA
CALIFORNIA BOARD OF LEGAL SPECIALIZATION

Law Offices of Brian D. Lerner

A PROFESSIONAL CORPORATION

CERTIFIED SPECIALIST IN IMMIGRATION AND NATIONALITY LAW
ADMITTED TO THE U.S. SUPREME COURT

LONG BEACH, CALIFORNIA
(562) 495-0554

CARSON, CALIFORNIA
(310) 684-5120

June 15, 2018

Premium Processing
USCIS Nebraska Service Center
850 S. Street
Lincoln, NE 68508

Re: Application: I-140, Immigrant Petition for Alien Worker
(Skilled Worker/Public Relations Specialist)
Petitioner: Consultants for America's ██████
Beneficiary: ██████

Dear Sir/Madam:

Consultants for ██████ (hereinafter "Petitioner") submits the following in support of its I-140, Immigrant Petition for Alien Worker, filed on behalf of ██████ (hereinafter "Beneficiary"), to classify her as a skilled worker pursuant to section 203(b)(3)(A)(i) of the Immigrant and Nationality Act (hereinafter "INA" or "Act"):

Forms	**Description**
G-28	Notice of Entry of Appearance as Attorney or Accredited Representative;
I-140	Immigrant Petition for Alien Worker and $700 Filing Fee; and
I-907	Request for Premium Processing Service and $1,225 Filing Fee.

Exhibits	**Description**
1.	Supporting Letter from Petitioner;
2.	Original Certified ETA Form 9089, Application for Permanent Employment Certification;
3.	Petitioner's Articles of Organization;
4.	Petitioner's Operating Agreement;
5.	Petitioner's IRS Employment Identification Number;
6.	Petitioner's 2016 Federal Income Tax Return;
7.	Petitioner's 2017 Federal Income Tax Return;
8.	O*Net Online – Public Relations Specialists;
9.	O*Net Online Job Zones Overview;
10.	O*Net Online Specific Vocational Preparation;
11.	Beneficiary's Birth Certificate;
12.	Beneficiary's Passport;
13.	Beneficiary's Curriculum Vitae/Resume; and
14.	Letters of Previous Employment for Beneficiary.

I.
PETITIONER'S I-140, IMMIGRANT PETITION FOR ALIEN WORKER, IS BEING TIMELY FILED.

Pursuant to 20 C.F.R. § 656.30 (b), an approved permanent labor certification granted on or after July 16, 2007, expires if not filed in support of a Form I-140 petition with the Department of Homeland Security within 180 calendar days of the date the Department of Labor granted the certification.

In the present case, the underlying ETA Form 9089, Application for Permanent Employment Certification, is valid from March 20, 2018 to September 16, 2018. Exhibit 2. Therefore, Petitioner's I-140 is being timely filed.

II.
THE POSITION OFFERED: PUBLIC RELATIONS SPECIALIST.

1. Skilled Workers.

Section 203(b)(3)(A) of the Act, provides in pertinent part:

> Visas shall be made available, in a number not to exceed 28.6 percent of such worldwide level, plus any visas not required for the classes specified in paragraphs (1) and (2), to the following classes of aliens who are not described in paragraph (2):
>
> (i) Skilled workers. - Qualified immigrants who are capable, at the time of petitioning for classification under this paragraph, of performing skilled labor (requiring at least 2 years training or experience), not of a temporary or seasonal nature, for which qualified workers are not available in the United States.
>
> (ii) Professionals. - Qualified immigrants who hold baccalaureate degrees and who are members of the professions.
>
> (iii) Other workers. - Other qualified immigrants who are capable, at the time of petitioning for classification under this paragraph, of performing unskilled labor, not of a temporary or seasonal nature, for which qualified workers are not available in the United States.

8 C.F.R. § 204.5 (l)(2) defines a "skilled worker" as:

> an alien who is capable, at the time of petitioning for this classification, of performing skilled labor (requiring at least two years training or experience), not of a temporary or seasonal nature, for which qualified workers are not available in the United States. Relevant post-secondary education may be considered as training for the purposes of this provision.

2. Public Relations Specialist.

In the present case, as indicated on the enclosed Application for Permanent Employment Certification (Form ETA 9089), the corresponding occupation title is Public Relations Specialist, with a corresponding Occupational Information network (O*NET) code of 27-3031. Exhibit 2.

The U.S. Department of Labor has certified the Application for Permanent Employment Certification, ETA Form 9089, and the original certified copy is enclosed herewith. Exhibit 2. The certification is ETA Case No. A-17296-01835, with validity from March 20, 2018 to September 16, 2018. Id. Having reviewed the Application for Permanent Employment Certification, including the specified job requirements, the U.S. Department of Labor has approved Petitioner's specified job requirements as the minimum requirements for the position. Given that the position requires, and the beneficiary possesses, more than two years of experience, clearly, the position and the beneficiary qualify for classification in the third employment-based preference category as a skilled worker.

3. Beneficiary Has The Necessary Two-Years Experience.

In the present case, Beneficiary has at least two-years experience in the following areas:

- Responding to requests for information about company/employer and its products and services;
- Preparing advertising, marketing and information materials to promote a company/employer and its products and services;
- Establishing or maintaining cooperative relationships with representatives of community, consumer, employee, or public interest groups;
- Planning or directing development or communication of programs to maintain favorable public perceptions of a company/employer and its products and services;
- Studying the objectives and needs of a company/employer to develop public relations strategies that will influence public opinion or promote ideas, products, or services;
- Updating and maintaining marketing, advertising and promotional materials;
- Conferring with management to identify trends, interests or concerns or identify potential clients;
- Arranging public appearances, lectures, contests, parties or exhibits to increase product or service awareness or to promote goodwill;
- Preparing or delivering presentations/speeches to further public relations objectives;
- Conferring with support personnel to produce or coordinate production of advertisements marketing or promotional material; and
- Consulting with advertising agencies or staff to arrange promotional campaigns.

Exhibits 2 and 13-14. This experience was gained primarily from Beneficiary's employment as a Marketing/PR Representative for Impact Company in Israel between February 2004 and January 2005 and her employment as a Guest Relations Representative for the [redacted] n Israel between December 2004 and March 2006. Exhibits 13-14. Accordingly, Beneficiary meets the requirements of the position and is qualified for the position and classification in the third employment-based preference category as a skilled worker.

III.
PETITIONER CAN PAY THE PREVAILING WAGE.

Pursuant to 8 C.F.R. § 204.5(g)(2), any petition filed by or for an employment-based immigrant who requires an offer of employment must be accompanied by evidence that the prospective United States employer has the ability to pay the proffered wage. The petitioner must demonstrate this ability at the time the priority date is established and continuing until the beneficiary obtains lawful permanent residence. Id. Generally, evidence of this ability must be either in the form of copies of annual reports, federal tax returns, or audited financial statements. Id.

In the present case, as indicated on ETA Form 9089, the proffered wage is $51,584. Exhibit 2. Further, as a sole proprietorship, Petitioner's 2016 Adjusted Gross Income was $127,930 and Petitioner's 2017 Ordinary Business Income was 292,837. Exhibit 6-7. Therefore, at the time of the filing of the Application for Permanent Employment Certification, Petitioner had, and still continues to have, the ability to pay the proffered wage.

IV.
CONCLUSION

Based on the foregoing, it is respectfully submitted that all of the necessary requirements have been properly met and complied with under the Act and the Code of Federal Regulations.

Therefore, we respectfully request that this petition be approved as soon as possible so that Beneficiary can apply for her immigrant visa and Petitioner can then employ her as a Public Relations Specialist.

If you should have any questions, please feel free to contact our office at (562) 495-0554.

Sincerely,

Brian D. Lerner
Attorney at Law

FORMS

Notice of Entry of Appearance as Attorney or Accredited Representative

Department of Homeland Security

DHS Form G-28
OMB No. 1615-0105
Expires 03/31/2018

Part 1. Information About Attorney or Accredited Representative

1. USCIS ELIS Account Number *(if any)* ►

Name and Address of Attorney or Accredited Representative

2.a. Family Name *(Last Name)*: Lerner
2.b. Given Name *(First Name)*: Brian
2.c. Middle Name: David
3.a. Street Number and Name: 3233 E Broadway
3.b. Apt. ☐ Ste. ☐ Flr. ☐
3.c. City or Town: Long Beach
3.d. State: CA 3.e. ZIP Code: 90803
3.f. Province:
3.g. Postal Code:
3.h. Country: USA
4. Daytime Telephone Number: 5624950554
5. Fax Number: 5626088672
6. E-Mail Address *(if any)*: blerner@californiaimmigration.us
7. Mobile Telephone Number *(if any)*:

Part 2. Notice of Appearance as Attorney or Accredited Representative

This appearance relates to immigration matters before *(Select only one box)*:

1.a. ☒ USCIS
1.b. List the form numbers: I-140
2.a. ☐ ICE
2.b. List the specific matter in which appearance is entered:
3.a. ☐ CBP
3.b. List the specific matter in which appearance is entered:

I enter my appearance as attorney or accredited representative at the request of:

4. Select **only one** box:
☐ Applicant ☒ Petitioner ☐ Requestor
☐ Respondent (ICE, CBP)

Information About Applicant, Petitioner, Requestor, or Respondent

5.a. Family Name *(Last Name)*: [redacted]
5.b. Given Name *(First Name)*: [redacted]
5.c. Middle Name: [redacted]
6. Name of Company or Organization *(if applicable)*: See Part 6

Part 2. Notice of Appearance as Attorney or Accredited Representative *(continued)*

Information About Applicant, Petitioner, Requestor, or Respondent (continued)

7. USCIS ELIS Account Number *(if any)*

▶

8. Alien Registration Number (A-Number) or Receipt Number

9. Daytime Telephone Number

10. Mobile Telephone Number *(if any)*

11. E-Mail Address *(if any)*

Mailing Address of Applicant, Petitioner, Requestor, or Respondent

NOTE: Provide the mailing address of the applicant, petitioner, requestor, or respondent. **Do not** provide the business mailing address of the attorney or accredited representative **unless** it serves as the safe mailing address on the application, petition, or request being filed with this Form G-28.

12.a. Street Number and Name

12.b. Apt. ☐ Ste. ☒ Flr. ☐

12.c. City or Town

12.d. State 12.e. ZIP Code

12.f. Province

12.g. Postal Code

12.h. Country

USA

Part 3. Eligibility Information for Attorney or Accredited Representative

Select all applicable items.

1.a. ☒ I am an attorney eligible to practice law in, and a member in good standing of, the bar of the highest courts of the following states, possessions, territories, commonwealths, or the District of Columbia. *(If you need additional space, use **Part 6.**)*

Licensing Authority

Supreme Court of California

1.b. Bar Number *(if applicable)*

158536

1.c. Name of Law Firm

Law Offices of Brian D. Lerner

1.d. I *(choose one)* ☒ *am not* ☐ *am*

subject to any order of any court or administrative agency disbarring, suspending, enjoining, restraining, or otherwise restricting me in the practice of law. If you are subject to any orders, explain in the space below. *(If you need additional space, use **Part 6.**)*

2.a. ☐ I am an accredited representative of the following qualified nonprofit religious, charitable, social service, or similar organization established in the United States, so recognized by the Department of Justice, Board of Immigration Appeals, in accordance with 8 CFR 292.2. Provide the name of the organization and the expiration date of accreditation.

2.b. Name of Recognized Organization

2.c. Date accreditation expires

(mm/dd/yyyy) ▶

Part 3. Eligibility Information for Attorney or Accredited Representative *(continued)*

3. ☐ I am associated with ______________________, the attorney or accredited representative of record who previously filed Form G-28 in this case, and my appearance as an attorney or accredited representative is at his or her request.

   NOTE: If you select this item, also complete **Item Numbers 1.a. - 1.b. or Item Numbers 2.a. - 2.c.** in **Part 3.** *(whichever is appropriate).*

4.a. ☐ I am a law student or law graduate working under the direct supervision of the attorney or accredited representative of record on this form in accordance with the requirements in 8 CFR 292.1(a)(2)(iv).

4.b. Name of Law Student or Law Graduate ______________________

Part 4. Applicant, Petitioner, Requestor, or Respondent Consent to Representation, Contact Information, and Signature

Consent to Representation and Release of Information

1. I have requested the representation of and consented to being represented by the attorney or accredited representative named in **Part 1.** of this form. According to the Privacy Act of 1974 and DHS policy, I also consent to the disclosure to the named attorney or accredited representative of any record pertaining to me that appears in any system of records of USCIS, ICE or CBP.

   When you (the applicant, petitioner, requestor, or respondent) are represented, DHS will send notices to both you and your attorney or accredited representative either through mail or electronic delivery.

   DHS will also send the Form I-94, Arrival Departure Record, to you **unless** you select **Item Number 2.a.** in **Part 4.** All secure identity documents and Travel Documents will be sent to you (the applicant, petitioner, requestor, or respondent) at your U.S. mailing address **unless** you ask us to send your secure identity documents to your attorney of record or accredited representative.

   If you do not want to receive original notices or secure identity documents directly, but would rather have such notices and documents sent to your attorney of record or accredited representative, please select **all applicable** boxes below:

2.a ☒ I request DHS send any notice (including Form I-94) on an application, petition, or request to the U.S. business address of my attorney of record or accredited representative as listed in this form. I understand that I may change this election at any future date through written notice to DHS.

2.b. ☐ I request that DHS send any secure identity document, such as a Permanent Resident Card, Employment Authorization Document, or Travel Document, that I am approved to receive and authorized to possess, to the U.S. business address of my attorney of record or accredited representative as listed in this form or to a designated military or diplomatic address for pickup in a foreign country (if permitted). I consent to having my secure identity document sent to my attorney of record or accredited representative's U.S. business address and understand that I may request, at any future date and through written notice to DHS, that DHS send any secure identity document to me directly.

3.a. Signature of Applicant, Petitioner, Requestor, or Respondent

➡ [signature]

3.b. Date of Signature *(mm/dd/yyyy)*► 05/02/2018

Part 5. Signature of Attorney or Accredited Representative

I have read and understand the regulations and conditions contained in 8 CFR 103.2 and 292 governing appearances and representation before the Department of Homeland Security. I declare under penalty of perjury under the laws of the United States that the information I have provided on this form is true and correct.

1. Signature of Attorney or Accredited Representative

   [signature]

2. Signature of Law Student or Law Graduate

   ____

3. Date of Signature *(mm/dd/yyyy)*► 05/02/2018

Part 6. Additional Information

Use the space provided below to provide additional information pertaining to **Part 3., Item Numbers 1.a. - 1.d.** or to provide your U.S. business address for purposes of receiving secure identity documents for your client (if your client has consented to your receipt of such documents under **Part 4.**)

Part 2.6 - Consultants for America's Veterans, LLC

Part 2.12.b - 10103

Immigrant Petition for Alien Worker

Department of Homeland Security
U.S. Citizenship and Immigration Services

USCIS
Form I-140
OMB No. 1615-0015
Expires 04/30/2018

For USCIS Use Only	Fee Stamp	Priority Date	Consulate	Action Block

Classification		Certification
☐ 203(b)(1)(A) Alien of Extraordinary Ability	☐ 203(b)(2) Member of Professions with Advanced Degree/Exceptional Ability	☐ National Interest Waiver (NIW)
☐ 203(b)(1)(B) Outstanding Professor or Researcher	☐ 203(b)(3)(A)(i) Skilled Worker	☐ Schedule A, Group I
☐ 203(b)(1)(C) Multinational Executive or Manager	☐ 203(b)(3)(A)(ii) Professional	☐ Schedule A, Group II
	☐ 203(b)(3)(A)(iii) Other Worker	Remarks

▶ **START HERE - Type or print in black ink.**

Part 1. Information About the Person or Organization Filing This Petition *(If an individual is filing, use numbers 1.a. - 1.c. If a Company or Organization is filing, use number 2).*

1.a. Family Name *(Last Name)* ████

1.b. Given Name *(First Name)* ████

1.c. Middle Name ████

2. Company or Organization Name
Consultants for America's Veterans, LLC

Other Information

3. IRS Tax Number *must be 9 digits; no dashes* ▶ ████

4. U.S. Social Security Number *(if any)* *must be 9 digits; no dashes* ▶

Mailing Address

5.a. In Care of Name

5.b. Street Number and Name ████

5.c. Apt. ☐ Ste. ☒ Flr. ☐ ████

5.d. City or Town ████

5.e. State ████ **5.f.** Zip Code ████

5.g. Postal Code

5.h. Province

5.i. Country
USA

Part 2. Petition Type

This petition is being filed for: (Select **only one** box):

1.a. ☐ An alien of extraordinary ability.

1.b. ☐ An outstanding professor or researcher.

1.c. ☐ A multinational executive or manager.

1.d. ☐ A member of the professions holding an advanced degree or an alien of exceptional ability (who is **NOT** seeking a National Interest Waiver).

1.e. ☐ A professional (at a minimum, possessing a bachelor's degree or a foreign degree equivalent to a U.S. bachelor's degree).

1.f. ☒ A skilled worker (requiring at least 2 years of specialized training or experience).

1.g. ☐ Any other worker (requiring less than 2 years of training or experience).

1.h. ☐ (Reserved)

1.i. ☐ An alien applying for a National Interest Waiver (who **IS** a member of the professions holding an advanced degree or an alien of exceptional ability).

Check below if this petition is being filed:

2.a. ☐ To amend a previously filed petition. Previous Petition Receipt Number: ▶

2.b. ☐ For the Schedule A, Group I or II designation.

Part 3. Information About the Person for Whom You Are Filing

1.a. Family Name *(Last Name)* [redacted]

1.b. Given Name *(First Name)* [redacted]

1.c. Middle Name

Mailing Address

2.a. In Care of Name [redacted]

2.b. Street Number and Name [redacted]

2.c. Apt. ☐ Ste. ☐ Flr. ☐

2.d. City or Town [redacted]

2.e. State 2.f. Zip Code

2.g. Postal Code [redacted]

2.h. Province

2.i. Country [redacted]

Other Information

3. E-mail Address *(if any)* [redacted]

4. Daytime Phone Number [redacted]

5. Date of Birth *(mm/dd/yyyy)* ▶ [redacted]

6. City/Town/Village of Birth [redacted]

7. State/Province of Birth [redacted]

8. Country of Birth [redacted]

9. Country of Citizenship [redacted]

10. Country of Nationality [redacted]

11. Alien Registration Number (A-Number)

▶ A-

12. U.S. Social Security Number *(if any)*
must be 9 digits; no dashes

▶ [redacted]

If in the United States, please provide the following (complete all sections, as applicable):

13. Date of Arrival *(mm/dd/yyyy)* ▶

14.a. I-94 Arrival-Departure Record Number:

▶

14.b. Passport Number

14.c. Travel Document Number

14.d. Country of Issuance for Passport or Travel Document

14.e. Expiration Date for Passport or Travel Document

(mm/dd/yyyy) ▶

15. Current Nonimmigrant Status

16. Date Status Expires:

(mm/dd/yyyy) ▶

Part 4. Processing Information

Complete the following for the person named in **Part 3**:
(Check one)

1.a. ☒ Alien will apply for a visa abroad at a U.S. Embassy or consulate at:

City or Town [redacted]

Country [redacted]

1.b. ☐ Alien is in the United States and will apply for adjustment of status to that of lawful permanent resident.

Alien's country of current residence or, if now in the United States, last country of permanent residence abroad.

Part 4. Processing Information *(continued)*

If you provided a United States address in **Part 3**, provide the person's foreign address:

2.a. Street Number and Name [ ]

2.b. Apt. ☐ Ste. ☐ Flr. ☐ [ ]

2.c. City or Town [ ]

2.d. Postal Code [ ]

2.e. Province [ ]

2.f. Country [ ]

If the person's native alphabet is other than Roman letters, write the person's foreign name and address in the native alphabet:

3.a. Family Name *(Last Name)* [ ]

3.b. Given Name *(First Name)* [ ]

3.c. Middle Name [ ]

Mailing Address

3.d. Street Number and Name [ ]

3.e. Apt. ☐ Ste. ☐ Flr. ☐ [ ]

3.f. City or Town [ ]

3.g. Postal Code [ ]

3.h. Province [ ]

3.i. Country [ ]

4. Are any other petition(s) or application(s) being filed with this Form I-140? ☐ Yes ☒ No

If you answered "**Yes**," check any applicable boxes:

☐ Form I-485

☐ Form I-131

☐ Form I-765

☐ Other-Attach an explanation

5. Is the person for whom you are filing in removal proceedings? ☐ Yes - Attach an explanation ☒ No

6. Has any immigrant visa petition ever been filed by or on behalf of this person? ☐ Yes - Attach an explanation ☒ No

7. Is the petition being filed without an original labor certification because the original labor certification was previously submitted in support of another Form I-140? ☐ Yes - Attach an explanation ☒ No

8. If the petition is being filed without an original labor certification, are you requesting that USCIS request a duplicate labor certification from the Department of Labor? ☐ Yes - Attach an explanation ☐ No

If you answered "Yes" to any of questions 4 through 8, provide the case number, office location, date of decision, and disposition of the decision on a separate sheet of paper.

Part 5. Additional Information About the Petitioner

Type of petitioner (Select **only one** box):

1.a. ☒ Employer

1.b. ☐ Self

1.c. ☐ Other (Explain, e.g., Permanent Resident, U.S. citizen or any other person filing on behalf of the alien) [ ]

If a company, give the following:

2.a. Type of Business: Consultant Firm

2.b. Date Established *(mm/dd/yyyy)* ▶ 01/31/2016

2.c. Current Number of U.S. Employees: 1

2.d. Gross Annual Income: 327,378

2.e. Net Annual Income: 292,837

2.f. NAICS Code ▶ [redacted]

2.g. Labor Certification DOL/ETA Case Number: [redacted]

Part 5. Additional Information About the Petitioner *(continued)*

2.h. Labor Certification DOL/ETA Filing Date

(mm/dd/yyyy) ▶ 10/23/2017

2.i. Labor Certification Expiration Date

(mm/dd/yyyy) ▶ 09/16/2018

If an individual, give following:

3.a. Occupation

3.b. Annual Income

Part 6. Basic Information About the Proposed Employment

1. Job Title: Public Relations Specialist

2. SOC Code ▶ 27 - 3031

3. Nontechnical Description of Job

See attachement.

4. Is this a full-time position? ☒ Yes ☐ No

5. If the answer to **Number 4** is "No," how many hours per week for the position?

6. Is this a permanent position? ☒ Yes ☐ No

7. Is this a new position? ☒ Yes ☐ No

8. Wages: $ $51, 584 per Year

(Specify hour, week, month, or year)

Address where the person will work if different from address in **Part 1.**

9.a. Street Number and Name

9.b. Apt. ☐ Ste. ☐ Flr. ☐

9.c. City or Town

9.d. State **9.e.** Zip Code

Part 7. Information on Spouse and All Children of the Person for Whom You Are Filing

List husband/wife and all children related to the individual for whom the petition is being filed. Also, note if the individual will be applying for a visa abroad or for adjustment of status as the dependent of the individual for whom the petition is filed. Provide an attachment of additional family members, if needed.

Person 1

1.a. Family Name *(Last Name)*

1.b. Given Name *(First Name)*

1.c. Middle Name

1.d. Date of Birth *(mm/dd/yyyy)* ▶

1.e. Country of Birth

1.f. Relationship

1.g. Applying for Adjustment of Status? ☐ Yes ☐ No

1.h. Applying for Visa Abroad? ☐ Yes ☐ No

Person 2

2.a. Family Name *(Last Name)*

2.b. Given Name *(First Name)*

2.c. Middle Name

2.d. Date of Birth *(mm/dd/yyyy)* ▶

2.e. Country of Birth

2.f. Relationship

2.g. Applying for Adjustment of Status? ☐ Yes ☐ No

2.h. Applying for Visa Abroad? ☐ Yes ☐ No

Part 7. Information on Spouse and All Children of the Person for Whom You Are Filing *(continued)*

Person 3

3.a. Family Name *(Last Name)*

3.b. Given Name *(First Name)*

3.c. Middle Name

3.d. Date of Birth *(mm/dd/yyyy)* ▶

3.e. Country of Birth

3.f. Relationship

3.g. Applying for Adjustment of Status? ☐ Yes ☐ No

3.h. Applying for Visa Abroad? ☐ Yes ☐ No

Person 4

4.a. Family Name *(Last Name)*

4.b. Given Name *(First Name)*

4.c. Middle Name

4.d. Date of Birth *(mm/dd/yyyy)* ▶

4.e. Country of Birth

4.f. Relationship

4.g. Applying for Adjustment of Status? ☐ Yes ☐ No

4.h. Applying for Visa Abroad? ☐ Yes ☐ No

Person 5

5.a. Family Name *(Last Name)*

5.b. Given Name *(First Name)*

5.c. Middle Name

5.d. Date of Birth *(mm/dd/yyyy)* ▶

5.e. Country of Birth

5.f. Relationship

5.g. Applying for Adjustment of Status? ☐ Yes ☐ No

5.h. Applying for Visa Abroad? ☐ Yes ☐ No

Person 6

6.a. Family Name *(Last Name)*

6.b. Given Name *(First Name)*

6.c. Middle Name

6.d. Date of Birth *(mm/dd/yyyy)* ▶

6.e. Country of Birth

6.f. Relationship

6.g. Applying for Adjustment of Status? ☐ Yes ☐ No

6.h. Applying for Visa Abroad? ☐ Yes ☐ No

Part 8. Signature of Petitioner

I certify, under penalty of perjury under the laws of the United States of America, that this petition and the evidence submitted with it are all true and correct. I authorize U.S. Citizenship and Immigration Services (USCIS) to release to other government agencies any information from my USCIS records, if USCIS determines that such action is necessary to determine eligibility for the benefit sought.

1.a. Signature of Petitioner

➡ [redacted]

1.b. Date of Signature *(mm/dd/yyyy)* ▶ 05/02/2018

2. Daytime Phone Number [redacted]

3. Mobile Phone Number [redacted]

4. E-mail Address *(if any)*

5. Job Title of Position with Petitioning Employer, If the Petition Is Being Filed by an Employer

NOTE: *If you do not fully complete this form or fail to submit the required documents listed in the instructions, a final decision on your petition may be delayed or the petition may be denied.*

Part 9. Signature of Person Preparing This Petition, If Other Than the Petitioner

1. Attorney or Representative: In the event of a Request for Evidence (RFE), may USCIS contact you by e-mail?

☒ Yes ☐ No

Preparer's Full Name

Provide the following information concerning the preparer:

2.a. Preparer's Family Name *(Last Name)*
Lerner

2.b. Preparer's Given Name *(First Name)*
Brian

3. Preparer's Business or Organization Name
Law Offices of Brian D. Lerner, APC

Preparer's Contact Information

4. Preparer's Daytime Phone Number (562) 495-0554 Extension

5. Preparer's E-mail Address *(if any)*
blerner@californiaimmigration.us

Preparer's Mailing Address

6.a. Street Number and Name: 3233 E. Broadway

6.b. Apt. ☐ Ste. ☐ Flr. ☐

6.c. City or Town: Long Beach

6.d. State: CA **6.e.** Zip Code: 90803

6.f. Postal Code

6.g. Province

6.h. Country: USA

Declaration

To be completed by all preparers, including attorneys and authorized representatives: I declare that I prepared this petition at the request of the petitioner, that it is based on all the information of which I have knowledge, and that the information is true to the best of my knowledge.

7.a. Signature of Preparer [signature]

7.b. Date of Signature *(mm/dd/yyyy)* ► 05/02/2018

Request for Premium Processing Service

Department of Homeland Security
U.S. Citizenship and Immigration Services

USCIS
Form I-907
OMB No. 1615-0048
Expires 01/31/2018

For USCIS Use Only	Request Physically Received by USCIS	Returned	Resubmitted	Receipt
	Date	Date	Date	
	Date	Date	Date	Action Block
	Remarks			

To be completed by an attorney or accredited representative (if any).	☒ Select this box if Form G-28 is attached.	Attorney State Bar Number (if applicable)	Attorney or Accredited Representative USCIS ELIS Account Number (if any)
		158536	

▶ START HERE - Type or print in black ink.

Part 1. Information About the Person Filing This Request

1. **Alien Registration Number (A-Number)** (if any)
   ▶ A-

2. **Family Name (Last Name)** [redacted] **Given Name (First Name)** [redacted] **Middle Name** [redacted]

3. **Company or Organization Named in the Related Case:** If filed on behalf of a company or organization
   Consultants for [redacted]

4. **Mailing Address**
   In Care Of Name

   Street Number and Name or PO Box Number [redacted]
   ☐ Apt. ☒ Ste. ☐ Flr. Number [redacted]

   City or Town [redacted] State [redacted] ZIP Code [redacted]

   Province Postal Code Country USA

5. Is your current mailing address the same as your physical address? ☒ Yes ☐ No

   If you answered "No," provide your physical address in **Item Number 6.**

Part 1. Information About the Person Filing This Request *(continued)*

6. Physical Address

Street Number and Name:

Apt. ☐ Ste. ☐ Flr. ☐ Number:

City or Town:

State:

ZIP Code:

Province:

Postal Code:

Country:

7. Request for Premium Processing Service: (select **only one** box)

☒ I am the **petitioner** who is filing or has filed a petition eligible for Premium Processing Service.

☐ I am the attorney or accredited representative **for the petitioner** who is filing or has filed a petition eligible for Premium Processing Service. (Complete and submit Form G-28, if Form G-28 has not been submitted with the petition.)

☐ I am the **applicant** who is filing or has filed an application eligible for Premium Processing Service.

☐ I am the attorney or accredited representative **for the applicant** who is filing or has filed an application eligible for Premium Processing Service. (Complete and submit Form G-28, if Form G-28 has not been submitted with the application.)

Part 2. Information About the Request

1. Form Number of Related Petition or Application

I-140

2. Receipt Number of Related Petition or Application

N/A

3. Classification or Eligibility Requested

EB-3

4. Petitioner or Applicant in the Related Case

Family Name (Last Name):

Given Name (First Name):

Middle Name:

5. Beneficiary in the Related Case

Family Name (Last Name):

Given Name (First Name):

Middle Name:

6. Name of Point of Contact for the Company or Organization

Family Name (Last Name):

Given Name (First Name):

Middle Name:

Position Title:

7. Company or Organization IRS Tax Number (if any)

Part 2. Information About the Request *(continued)*

8. Address of Petitioner, Applicant, Company or Organization Named in Related Case

Street Number and Name: [redacted]

Apt. ☐ Ste. ☒ Flr. ☐ Number: [redacted]

City or Town: [redacted]

State: [redacted] ZIP Code: [redacted]

Province:

Postal Code:

Country: USA

Part 3. Requestor's Statement, Certification, Signature, and Contact Information

I understand that U.S. Citizenship and Immigration Services (USCIS) will refund the Premium Processing Service fee to the person listed in **Part 1.** of this request if USCIS does not take an action on the related case within 15 calendar days after the appropriate USCIS office physically receives this request. I understand that case actions include a referral for investigation of suspected fraud or misrepresentation, or the issuance of:

1. An approval notice;
2. A request for evidence;
3. A notice of intent to deny; or
4. A denial notice.

Requestor's Statement

NOTE: Select the box for either **Item A.** or **B.** in **Item Number 1.** If applicable, select the box for **Item Number 2.**

1. Requestor's Statement Regarding the Interpreter

A. ☒ I can read and understand English, and have read and understand each and every question and instruction on this request, as well as my answer to each question.

B. ☐ The interpreter named in **Part 4.** has read to me each and every question and instruction on this request, as well as my answer to each question, in ________, a language in which I am fluent. I understand each and every question and instruction on this request as translated to me by my interpreter, and have provided true and correct responses in the language indicated above.

2. Requestor's Statement Regarding the Preparer

☒ I have requested the services of and consented to Brian D. Lerner, ☒ who is ☐ is not an attorney or accredited representative, preparing this request for me.

Requestor's Certification

I certify, under penalty of perjury under the laws of the United States of America, that the information in my request and any document submitted with my request is complete, true and correct.

Copies of any documents I have submitted are exact photocopies of unaltered, original documents, and I understand that USCIS may require that I submit original documents to USCIS at a later date. Furthermore, I authorize the release of any information from my records that USCIS may need to determine my eligibility for the immigration benefit that I seek.

I furthermore authorize release of information contained in this request and in supporting documents, and in my USCIS records, to other entities and persons where necessary for the administration of U.S. immigration laws.

Part 3. Requestor's Statement, Certification, Signature, and Contact Information *(continued)*

Requestor's Signature

3. Requestor's Signature [redacted]

Date of Signature (mm/dd/yyyy) ▶ 05/02/2018

Requestor's Contact Information

4. Requestor's Daytime Telephone Number [redacted]

5. Requestor's Mobile Telephone Number (if any) [redacted]

6. Requestor's Email Address (if any) [redacted]

7. Requestor's Fax Number (if any) [redacted]

Part 4. Interpreter's Contact Information, Certification, and Signature

Provide the following information about the interpreter:

Interpreter's Full Name

1. Interpreter's Family Name (Last Name)

Interpreter's Given Name (First Name)

2. Interpreter's Business or Organization Name (if any)

Interpreter's Mailing Address

3. Street Number and Name

Apt. ☐ Ste. ☐ Flr. ☐ Number

City or Town

State

ZIP Code

Province

Postal Code

Country

Interpreter's Contact Information

4. Interpreter's Daytime Telephone Number

5. Interpreter's Email Address (if any)

Interpreter's Certification

I certify that:

I am fluent in English and ________, which is the same language provided in **Part 3., Item B.** in **Item Number 1.**;

I have read to this requestor each and every question and instruction on this request, as well as the answer to each question, in the language provided in **Part 3., Item B.** in **Item Number 1.**; and

The requestor has informed me that they understand each and every instruction and question on the request, as well as their answer to each question.

Part 4. Interpreter's Contact Information, Certification, and Signature *(continued)*

Interpreter's Signature

6. **Interpreter's Signature** | **Date of Signature** (mm/dd/yyyy) ►

Part 5. Name, Contact Information, Declaration, and Signature of the Person Preparing this Request, If Other Than the Requestor

Provide the following information about the preparer:

Preparer's Full Name

1. **Preparer's Family Name (Last Name)**: Lerner
   Preparer's Given Name (First Name): Brian
2. **Preparer's Business or Organization Name (if any)**: Law Offices of Brian D. Lerner, APC

Preparer's Mailing Address

3. **Street Number and Name**: 3233 E. Broadway
   Apt. ☐ **Ste.** ☐ **Flr.** ☐ **Number**:
   City or Town: Long Beach
   State: CA
   ZIP Code: 90803
   Province:
   Postal Code:
   Country: USA

Preparer's Contact information

4. **Preparer's Telephone Number**: (562) 495-0554
5. **Preparer's Fax Number**: (562) 608-8672
6. **Preparer's Email Address (if any)**: blerner@californiaimmigration.us

Preparer's Statement

7.A. ☐ I am not an attorney or accredited representative but have prepared this request on behalf of the requestor with the requestor's consent.

7.B. ☒ I am an attorney or accredited representative and my representation of the requestor in this case (choose one) ☒ extends ☐ does not extend beyond the preparation of this request.

Part 5. Name, Contact Information, Declaration, and Signature of the Person Preparing this Request, If Other Than the Requestor *(continued)*

Preparer's Declaration

By my signature, I certify, swear or affirm, under penalty of perjury, that I prepared this request on behalf of, at the request of, and with the express consent of, the requestor. I completed the request based only on responses the requestor provided to me. After completing the request, I reviewed it and all of the requestor's responses with the requestor, who agreed with each and every answer provided for each question on the request and, when required, supplied additional information to respond to a question on the request.

Preparer's Signature

8. Preparer's Signature

Date of Signature (mm/dd/yyyy) ► 05/02/2018

EXHIBITS

EXHIBIT #1

Consultant’s Support Letter

CONSULTANTS FOR AMERICA'S VETERANS, LLC.

Consultation and representation for America's Veterans, their families, and organizations who care for them!

May 22, 2018

U.S. Citizenship and Immigration Services
Attn: I-140
2501 S. State Highway 121, Business Suite 400
Lewisville, TX 75067

Re: I-140, Immigrant Petition for Alien Worker
Beneficiary:

To Whom It May Concern:

Consultants ubmit this letter in support of our I-140, Petition for Alien Worker, filed on behalf Ms. ıeli national, so that can be employed by our company as a Public Relations Specialist.

Our company, established in 2016 by DrPH, MACM, MHA, a U.S. military veteran, is dedicated to helping U.S. Military Veterans and Servicemembers, their families, and organizations that care for them by providing services to enhance the quality of life for our veterans. Our services include VA accredited representation training and education; preparation, presentation, and prosecution of claims and appeals for U.S. Department of Veterans Affairs benefits, and consulting services for veterans, their families, and organizations that care for them. Some of our consulting services included financial accounting services; VA home loans; web-development, SEO, marketing, and graphic design; pre-employment and life coaching; and even professional wedding photography and make-up artistry.

As an addition to our company, we seek to employ as a Public Relations Specialist. In that capacity, her duties will include: responding to requests for information about our company and our services; preparing advertising, marketing and information materials to promote our company and our services; establishing and maintaining cooperative relationships with representatives of community, consumers, employees, and public interest groups, including various U.S. Embassies throughout the world; planning and directing development and communication of programs to maintain a favorable public perception of our company and our services; studying the objectives and needs of our company to develop public relations strategies that will influence public opinion or promote ideas, products, and services; updating and maintaining marketing, advertising and promotional materials for our company; conferring with management to identify trends, interests or concerns and identify potential new clients; arranging public appearances, lectures, contests, parties or exhibits to increase service awareness and to promote goodwill; preparing or delivering presentations/speeches to further public relations objectives; conferring with support personnel to produce or coordinate production of advertisements, marketing and promotional material; and consulting with advertising agencies or staff to arrange promotional campaigns.

Our goal, with is to dramatically increase our reach both domestically and internationally.

CONSULTANTS FOR AMERICA'S VETERANS, LLC.

Consultation and representation for America's Veterans, their families, and organizations who care for them!

It is our intention to employ [redacted] a permanent basis. She will work full-time, 40-hours a week, for our company in [redacted] with a yearly salary of $51,584.

Based upon [redacted] qualifications and two-years related experience, we are confident that she will be more than qualified for the position being offered by our company and therefore, respectfully request that our I-140 be approved accordingly.

Rudy S. Melson, President & Founder
Consultants for America's Veterans, LLC

EXHIBIT #2

U.S. Department of Labor Letter Certification

U.S. Department of Labor

Employment and Training Administration
Office of Foreign Labor Certification
Atlanta National Processing Center
Harris Tower
233 Peachtree Street, Suite 410
Atlanta, GA 30303

March 20, 2018

CONSULTANTS FOR AMERICA'S

c/o Law Offices of Brian D. Lerner, APC
Brian D. Lerner
3233 E. Broadway
Long Beach, CA 90803

ETA Case Number:
Foreign Worker's Name:
Occupation Title:

Occupation Code:
Priority Date:

Dear CONSULTANTS

The United States Department of Labor has made a determination on your Application for Permanent Employment Certification (ETA Form 9089) pursuant to Departmental regulations at 20 CFR §656.24 and as required by the Immigration and Nationality Act, as amended.

Form ETA 9089 has been certified and is enclosed. This certification must be attached to the I-140 petition and filed with the appropriate office of the United States Citizenship and Immigration Services.

Sincerely,

PERM Certifying Officer

Enclosure(s): ETA Form 9089

EXHIBIT #3

ETA Form 9089

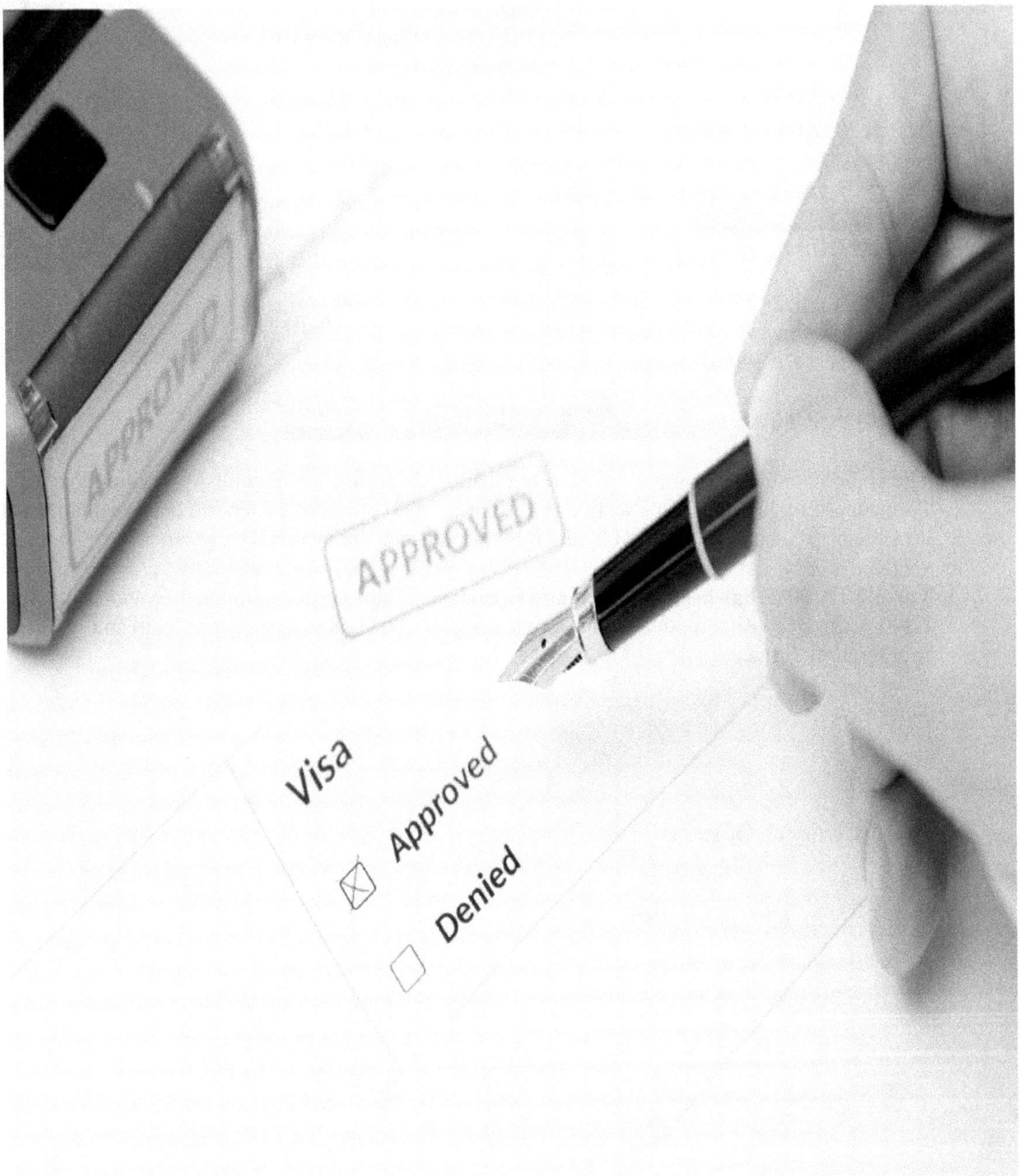

OMB Approval: 1205-0451
Expiration Date: 03/31/2018

Application for Permanent Employment Certification

ETA Form 9089

U.S. Department of Labor

Please read and review the filing instructions before completing this form. A copy of the instructions can be found at http://www.foreignlaborcert.doleta.gov/pdf/9089inst.pdf

Employing or continuing to employ an alien unauthorized to work in the United States is illegal and may subject the employer to criminal prosecution, civil money penalties, or both.

A. Refiling Instructions

1. Are you seeking to utilize the filing date from a previously submitted Application for Alien Employment Certification (ETA 750)?	☐ Yes ☑ No
1-A. If Yes, enter the previous filing date	
1-B. Indicate the previous SWA or local office case number OR if not available, specify state where case was originally filed:	

B. Schedule A or Sheepherder Information

1. Is this application in support of a Schedule A or Sheepherder Occupation?	☐ Yes ☑ No
If Yes, do NOT send this application to the Department of Labor. All applications in support of Schedule A or Sheepherder Occupations must be sent directly to the appropriate Department of Homeland Security office.	

C. Employer Information (Headquarters or Main Office)

1. Employer's name CONSULTANTS FOR ████ LLC			
2. Address 1 ████			
Address 2 ████			
3. City ████	State/Province ████	Country UNITED STATES OF AMERICA	Postal code 92123
4. Phone number ████		Extension	
5. Number of employees 1		6. Year commenced business 2016	
7. FEIN(Federal Employer Identification Number) ████		8. NAICS Code 611710	
9. Is the employer a closely held corporation, partnership, or sole proprietorship in which the alien has an ownership interest, or is there a familial relationship between the owners, stockholders, partners, corporate officers, or incorporators, and the alien?		☐ Yes ☑ No	

D. Employer Contact Information (This section must be filled out. This information must be different from the agent or attorney information listed in Section E).

1. Contact's last name ████	First name ████		Middle initial S
2. Address 1 ████			
Address 2 ████			
3. City ████	State/Province CA	Country UNITED STATES OF AMERICA	Postal code 92123
4. Phone number ████		Extension	
5. E-mail address ████			

E. Agent or Attorney Information (If applicable)

1. Agent or attorney's last name: Lerner | First name: Brian | Middle initial: D
2. Firm name: Law Offices of Brian D. Lerner, APC
3. Firm EIN: 331012936 | 4. Phone number: 5624950554 | Extension:
5. Address 1: 3233 E. Broadway
   Address 2:
6. City: Long Beach | State/Province: CA | Country: UNITED STATES OF AMERICA | Postal code: 90803
7. E-mail address: blerner@californiaimmigration.us

F. Prevailing Wage Information (as provided by the State Workforce Agency)

1. Prevailing wage tracking number (if applicable): P-100-16326-878 | 2. SOC/O*NET(OES) code: 27-3031
3. Occupation Title: Public Relations Specialist | 4. Skill Level: Level II
5. Prevailing wage: $ 51,584.00 | Per: (Choose only one) ☐ Hour ☐ Week ☐ Bi-Weekly ☐ Month ☑ Year
6. Prevailing wage source (Choose only one): ☑ OES ☐ CBA ☐ Employer Conducted Survey ☐ DBA ☐ SCA ☐ Other
6-A. If Other is indicated in question 6, specify:
7. Determination date: 04/25/2017 | 8. Expiration date: 07/24/2017

G. Wage Offer Information

1. Offered wage
   From: $ 51,584.00 | To: (Optional) $ | Per: (Choose only one) ☐ Hour ☐ Week ☐ Bi-Weekly ☐ Month ☑ Year

H. Job Opportunity Information (Where work will be performed)

1. Primary worksite (where work is to be performed) address 1: [redacted]
   Address 2: [redacted]
2. City: [redacted] | State: [redacted] | Postal code: [redacted]
3. Job title: [redacted]
4. Education: minimum level required:
   ☐ None ☐ High School ☐ Associate's ☑ Bachelor's ☐ Master's ☐ Doctorate ☐ Other
4-A. If Other is indicated in question 4, specify the education required:
4-B. Major field of study: Public Relations, Communications, Etc.
5. Is training required for the job opportunity? ☐ Yes ☑ No | 5-A. If Yes, number of months of training required:

ETA Case Number: [redacted]

H. Job Opportunity Information Continued

5-B. Indicate the field of training:

6. Is experience in the job offered required for the job? [✓] Yes [ ] No
6-A. If Yes, number of months experience required: 3

7. Is there an alternate field of study that is acceptable? [ ] Yes [✓] No

7-A. If Yes, specify the major field of study:

8. Is there an alternate combination of education and experience that is acceptable? [✓] Yes [ ] No

8-A. If Yes, specify the alternate level of education required:
[ ] None [ ] High School [ ] Associate's [ ] Bachelor's [ ] Master's [ ] Doctorate [✓] Other

8-B. If Other is indicated in question 8-A, indicate the alternate level of education required:
High School plus 2 Years Related Experience

8-C. If applicable, indicate the number of years experience acceptable in question 8:
2

9. Is a foreign educational equivalent acceptable? [✓] Yes [ ] No

10. Is experience in an alternate occupation acceptable? [ ] Yes [✓] No
10-A. If Yes, number of months experience in alternate occupation required:

10-B. Identify the job title of the acceptable alternate occupation:

11. Job duties – If submitting by mail, add attachment if necessary. Job duties description must begin in this space.
See Attachment

12. Are the job opportunity's requirements normal for the occupation? [✓] Yes [ ] No

If the answer to this question is No, the employer must be prepared to provide documentation demonstrating that the job requirements are supported by business necessity.

13. Is knowledge of a foreign language required to perform the job duties? [ ] Yes [✓] No

If the answer to this question is Yes, the employer must be prepared to provide documentation demonstrating that the language requirements are supported by business necessity.

14. Specific skills or other requirements – If submitting by mail, add attachment if necessary. Skills description must begin in this space.
See Attachment

H. Job Opportunity Information Continued

15. Does this application involve a job opportunity that includes a combination of occupations?	☐ Yes ☑ No
16. Is the position identified in this application being offered to the alien identified in Section J?	☑ Yes ☐ No
17. Does the job require the alien to live on the employer's premises?	☐ Yes ☑ No
18. Is the application for a live-in household domestic service worker?	☐ Yes ☑ No
18-A. If Yes, have the employer and the alien executed the required employment contract and has the employer provided a copy of the contract to the alien?	☐ Yes ☐ No ☐ NA

I. Recruitment Information

a. Occupation Type – All must complete this section.

1. Is this application for a **professional occupation**, other than a college or university teacher? Professional occupations are those for which a bachelor's degree (or equivalent) is normally required.	☑ Yes ☐ No
2. Is this application for a college or university teacher? **If Yes, complete questions 2-A and 2-B below.**	☐ Yes ☑ No
2-A. Did you select the candidate using a competitive recruitment and selection process?	☐ Yes ☐ No
2-B. Did you use the basic recruitment process for professional occupations?	☐ Yes ☐ No

b. Special Recruitment and Documentation Procedures for College and University Teachers – Complete only if the answer to question I.a.2-A is Yes.

3. Date alien selected:
4. Name and date of national professional journal in which advertisement was placed:
5. Specify additional recruitment information in this space. Add an attachment if necessary.

c. Professional/Non-Professional Information – Complete this section unless your answer to question B.1 or I.a.2-A is YES.

6. Start date for the SWA job order 07/17/2017	7. End date for the SWA job order 09/06/2017
8. Is there a Sunday edition of the newspaper in the area of intended employment?	☑ Yes ☐ No
9. Name of newspaper (of general circulation) in which the first advertisement was placed: San Diego Union Tribune	
10. Date of first advertisement identified in question 9: 07/09/2017	
11. Name of newspaper or professional journal (if applicable) in which second advertisement was placed: San Diego Union Tribune	☑ Newspaper ☐ Journal

I. Recruitment Information Continued

12. Date of second newspaper advertisement or date of publication of journal identified in question 11: 07/16/2017

d. Professional Recruitment Information – Complete if the answer to question I.a.1 is YES or if the answer to I.a.2-B is YES. Complete at least 3 of the items.

13. Dates advertised at job fair From: To:	14. Dates of on-campus recruiting From: To:
15. Dates posted on employer web site From: 07/18/2017 To: 09/11/2017	16. Dates advertised with trade or professional organization From: To:
17. Dates listed with job search web site From: 07/19/2017 To: 07/20/2017	18. Dates listed with private employment firm From: To:
19. Dates advertised with employee referral program From: To:	20. Dates advertised with campus placement office From: To:
21. Dates advertised with local or ethnic newspaper From: 07/27/2017 To: 08/02/2017	22. Dates advertised with radio or TV ads From: To:

e. General Information – All must complete this section.

23. Has the employer received payment of any kind for the submission of this application?	☐ Yes ☑ No
23-A. If Yes, describe details of the payment including the amount, date and purpose of the payment :	
24. Has the bargaining representative for workers in the occupation in which the alien will be employed been provided with notice of this filing at least 30 days but not more than 180 days before the date the application is filed?	☐ Yes ☐ No ☑ NA
25. If there is no bargaining representative, has a notice of this filing been posted for 10 business days in a conspicuous location at the place of employment, ending at least 30 days before but not more than 180 days before the date the application is filed?	☑ Yes ☐ No ☐ NA
26. Has the employer had a layoff in the area of intended employment in the occupation involved in this application or in a related occupation within the six months immediately preceding the filing of this application?	☐ Yes ☑ No
26-A. If Yes, were the laid off U.S. workers notified and considered for the job opportunity for which certification is sought?	☐ Yes ☐ No ☐ NA

J. Alien Information (This section must be filled out. This information must be different from the agent or attorney information listed in Section E).

1. Alien's last name [redacted]	First name [redacted]	Full middle name	
2. Current address 1 [redacted]			
Address 2			
3. City [redacted]	State/Province	Country [redacted]	Postal code 68101
4. Phone number of current residence [redacted]			
5. Country of citizenship [redacted]		6. Country of birth [redacted]	
7. Alien's date of birth [redacted]		8. Class of admission Not in USA	
9. Alien registration number (A#)		10. Alien admission number (I-94)	

11. Education: highest level achieved as required by the requested job opportunity:

☐ None ☑ High School ☐ Associate's ☐ Bachelor's ☐ Master's ☐ Doctorate ☐ Other

J. Alien Information Continued

11-A. If Other indicated in question 11, specify	
12. Specify major field(s) of study	
13. Year relevant education completed 2001	
14. Institution where relevant education specified in question 11 was received	
15. Address 1 of conferring institution	
Address 2	
16. City / State/Province / Country / Postal code	
17. Did the alien complete the training required for the requested job opportunity, as indicated in question H.5?	☐ Yes ☐ No ☑ NA
18. Does the alien have the experience as required for the requested job opportunity indicated in question H.6?	☑ Yes ☐ No ☐ NA
19. Does the alien possess the alternate combination of education and experience as indicated in question H.8?	☑ Yes ☐ No ☐ NA
20. Does the alien have the experience in an alternate occupation specified in question H.10?	☐ Yes ☐ No ☑ NA
21. Did the alien gain any of the qualifying experience with the employer in a position substantially comparable to the job opportunity requested?	☐ Yes ☑ No ☐ NA
22. Did the employer pay for any of the alien's education or training necessary to satisfy any of the employer's job requirements for this position?	☐ Yes ☑ No
23. Is the alien currently employed by the petitioning employer?	☑ Yes ☐ No

K. Alien Work Experience

List all jobs the alien has held during the past 3 years. Also list any other experience that qualifies the alien for the job opportunity for which the employer is seeking certification.

a. Job 1

1. Employer name Consulate General of Israel			
2. Address 1 [redacted]			
Address 2			
3. City Los Angeles	State/Province CA	Country UNITED STATES OF AMERICA	Postal code 90025
4. Type of business Consulate		5. Job title Consular Assistant	
6. Start date 05/01/2012	7. End date 04/28/2017	8. Number of hours worked per week 35	

Job 1 continued on next page

K. Alien Work Experience Continued

9. Job details (duties performed, use of tools, machines, equipment, skills, qualifications, certifications, licenses, etc. Include the phone number of the employer and the name of the alien's supervisor.)

See Attachment

b. Job 2

1. Employer name [redacted]			
2. Address 1 [redacted]			
Address 2			
3. City [redacted]	State/Province [redacted]	Country	Postal code 61501
4. Type of business [redacted]		5. Job title Guest Relations Represent:	
6. Start date 12/01/2004	7. End date 04/30/2006	8. Number of hours worked per week 45	

9. Job details (duties performed, use of tools, machines, equipment, skills, qualifications, certifications, licenses, etc. Include the phone number of the employer and the name of the alien's supervisor.)

See Attachment

c. Job 3

1. Employer name [redacted]			
2. Address 1 [redacted]			
Address 2			
3. City Tel Aviv	State/Province	Country ISRAEL	Postal code 6380501
4. Type of business PR and Marketing company		5. Job title Marketing Representative	
6. Start date 02/01/2004	7. End date 01/30/2005	8. Number of hours worked per week 45	

Job 3 continued on next page

K. Alien Work Experience Continued

9. Job details (duties performed, use of tools, machines, equipment, skills, qualifications, certifications, licenses, etc. Include the phone number of the employer and the name of the alien's supervisor.)

See Attachment

L. Alien Declaration

I declare under penalty of perjury that Sections J and K are true and correct. *I understand that to knowingly furnish false information in the preparation of this form and any supplement thereto or to aid, abet, or counsel another to do so is a federal offense punishable by a fine or imprisonment up to five years or both under 18 U.S.C. §§ 2 and 1001. Other penalties apply as well to fraud or misuse of ETA immigration documents and to perjury with respect to such documents under 18 U.S.C. §§ 1546 and 1621.*

In addition, I ***further declare*** *under penalty of perjury that I intend to accept the position offered in Section H of this application if a labor certification is approved and I am granted a visa or an adjustment of status based on this application.*

1. Alien's last name	First name	Full middle name
[redacted]	[redacted]	
2. Signature	Date signed June 10th 2018	

Note – The signature and date signed do not have to be filled out when electronically submitting to the Department of Labor for processing, but must be complete when submitting by mail. If the application is submitted electronically, any resulting certification MUST be signed *immediately upon receipt* from DOL before it can be submitted to USCIS for final processing.

M. Declaration of Preparer

1. **Was the application completed by the employer?** If No, you must complete this section.	☐ Yes	☑ No

I hereby certify that I have prepared this application at the direct request of the employer listed in Section C and that to the best of my knowledge the information contained herein is true and correct. *I understand that to knowingly furnish false information in the preparation of this form and any supplement thereto or to aid, abet, or counsel another to do so is a federal offense punishable by a fine, imprisonment up to five years or both under 18 U.S.C. §§ 2 and 1001. Other penalties apply as well to fraud or misuse of ETA immigration documents and to perjury with respect to such documents under 18 U.S.C. §§ 1546 and 1621.*

2. Preparer's last name	First name	Middle initial
Lerner	Brian	D
3. Title		
Attorney		
4. E-mail address		
blerner@californiaimmigration.us		
5. Signature	Date signed 6/11/18	

Note – The signature and date signed do not have to be filled out when electronically submitting to the Department of Labor for processing, but must be complete when submitting by mail. If the application is submitted electronically, any resulting certification MUST be signed *immediately upon receipt* from DOL before it can be submitted to USCIS for final processing.

N. Employer Declaration

By virtue of my signature below, ***I HEREBY CERTIFY*** *the following conditions of employment:*

1. The offered wage equals or exceeds the prevailing wage and I will pay at least the prevailing wage.
2. The wage is not based on commissions, bonuses or other incentives, unless I guarantees a wage paid on a weekly, bi-weekly, or monthly basis that equals or exceeds the prevailing wage.
3. I have enough funds available to pay the wage or salary offered the alien.
4. I will be able to place the alien on the payroll on or before the date of the alien's proposed entrance into the United States.
5. The job opportunity does not involve unlawful discrimination by race, creed, color, national origin, age, sex, religion, handicap, or citizenship.
6. The job opportunity is not:
   a. Vacant because the former occupant is on strike or is being locked out in the course of a labor dispute involving a work stoppage; or
   b. At issue in a labor dispute involving a work stoppage.
7. The job opportunity's terms, conditions, and occupational environment are not contrary to Federal, state or local law.
8. The job opportunity has been and is clearly open to any U.S. worker.
9. The U.S. workers who applied for the job opportunity were rejected for lawful job-related reasons.
10. The job opportunity is for full-time, permanent employment for an employer other than the alien.

I hereby designate the agent or attorney identified in section E (if any) to represent me for the purpose of labor certification and, by virtue of my signature in Block 3 below, **I take full responsibility** for the accuracy of any representations made by my agent or attorney.

I declare under penalty of perjury that I have read and reviewed this application and that to the best of my knowledge the information contained herein is true and accurate. *I understand that to knowingly furnish false information in the preparation of this form and any supplement thereto or to aid, abet, or counsel another to do so is a federal offense punishable by a fine or imprisonment up to five years or both under 18 U.S.C. §§ 2 and 1001. Other penalties apply as well to fraud or misuse of ETA immigration documents and to perjury with respect to such documents under 18 U.S.C. §§ 1546 and 1621.*

1. Last name	First name	Middle initial
[redacted]	[redacted]	S
2. Title President and Founder		
3. Signature [signature]	Date signed 5/15/18	

Note – The signature and date signed do not have to be filled out when electronically submitting to the Department of Labor for processing, but must be complete when submitting by mail. If the application is submitted electronically, any resulting certification MUST be signed *immediately upon receipt* from DOL before it can be submitted to USCIS for final processing.

O. U.S. Government Agency Use Only

Pursuant to the provisions of Section 212 (a)(5)(A) of the Immigration and Nationality Act, as amended, I hereby certify that there are not sufficient U.S. workers available and the employment of the above will not adversely affect the wages and working conditions of workers in the U.S. similarly employed.

This Certification is valid from 03/20/2018 to 09/16/2018

Certifying Officer
Signature of Certifying Officer — Date

03/20/2018
Signed

Case Number

10/23/2017
Filing Date

P. OMB Information *Paperwork Reduction Act Information Control Number 1205-0451*

Persons are not required to respond to this collection of information unless it displays a currently valid OMB control number.

Respondent's reply to these reporting requirements is required to obtain the benefits of permanent employment certification (Immigration and Nationality Act, Section 212(a)(5)). Public reporting burden for this collection of information is estimated to average 1¼ hours per response, including the time for reviewing instructions, searching existing data sources, gathering and maintaining the data needed, and completing and reviewing the collection of information. Send comments regarding this burden estimate to the Division of Foreign Labor Certification * U.S. Department of Labor * Room C4312 * 200 Constitution Ave., NW * Washington, DC * 20210.

Do NOT send the completed application to this address.

Q. Privacy Statement Information

In accordance with the Privacy Act of 1974, as amended (5 U.S.C. 552a), you are hereby notified that the information provided herein is protected under the Privacy Act. The Department of Labor (Department or DOL) maintains a System of Records titled Employer Application and Attestation File for Permanent and Temporary Alien Workers (DOL/ETA-7) that includes this record.

Under routine uses for this system of records, case files developed in processing labor certification applications, labor condition applications, or labor attestations may be released as follows: in connection with appeals of denials before the DOL Office of Administrative Law Judges and Federal courts, records may be released to the employers that filed such applications, their representatives, to named alien beneficiaries or their representatives, and to the DOL Office of Administrative Law Judges and Federal courts; and in connection with administering and enforcing immigration laws and regulations, records may be released to such agencies as the DOL Office of Inspector General, Employment Standards Administration, the Department of Homeland Security, and the Department of State.

Further relevant disclosures may be made in accordance with the Privacy Act and under the following circumstances: in connection with federal litigation; for law enforcement purposes; to authorized parent locator persons under Pub. L. 93-647; to an information source or public authority in connection with personnel, security clearance, procurement, or benefit-related matters; to a contractor or their employees, grantees or their employees, consultants, or volunteers who have been engaged to assist the agency in the performance of Federal activities; for Federal debt collection purposes; to the Office of Management and Budget in connection with its legislative review, coordination, and clearance activities; to a Member of Congress or their staff in response to an inquiry of the Congressional office made at the written request of the subject of the record; in connection with records management; and to the news media and the public when a matter under investigation becomes public knowledge, the Solicitor of Labor determines the disclosure is necessary to preserve confidence in the integrity of the Department, or the Solicitor of Labor determines that a legitimate public interest exists in the disclosure of information, unless the Solicitor of Labor determines that disclosure would constitute an unwarranted invasion of personal privacy.

Addendum

H. 11. Job duties

Responding to requests for information about company and its products and services; Preparing advertising, marketing and information materials to promote a company and its products and services; Establishing or maintaining cooperative relationships with representatives of community, consumer, employee, or public interest groups; Planning or directing, development or communication of programs to maintain favorable public perceptions of a company and its products and services; Studying the objectives and needs of a company to develop public relations strategies that will influence public opinion or promote ideas, products, or services; Updating and maintaining marketing, advertising and promotional materials; Conferring with management to identify trends, interests or concerns or identify potential clients; Arranging public appearances, lectures, contests, parties or exhibits to increase product or service awareness or to promote goodwill; Preparing or delivering presentations/speeches to further public relations objectives; Conferring with support personnel to produce or coordinate production of advertisements marketing or promotional material; and Consulting with advertising agencies or staff to arrange promotional campaigns.

Addendum

H. 14. Specific skills or other requirements

Responding to requests for information about company/employer and its products and services; Preparing advertising, marketing and information materials to promote a company/employer and its products and services; Establishing or maintaining cooperative relationships with representatives of community, consumer, employee, or public interest groups; Planning or directing development or communication of programs to maintain favorable public perceptions of a company/employer and its
products and services; Studying the objectives and needs of a company/employer to develop public relations strategies that will influence public opinion or promote ideas, products, or services;
Updating and maintaining marketing, advertising and promotional materials; Conferring with management to identify trends, interests or concerns or identify potential clients; Arranging public appearances, lectures, contests, parties or exhibits to increase product or service awareness or to
promote goodwill; Preparing or delivering presentations/speeches to further public relations objectives; Conferring with support personnel to produce or coordinate production of advertisements marketing or promotional material; and Consulting with advertising agencies or staff
to arrange promotional campaigns.

Addendum

K. 9. Job 1 - Job Details

Providing information about the consulte's services; Training both existing and new employees; Dealing with high volume of clients with different needs and directing or providing them with the relevant service providers/ organizations; Preparing, examining and approving variety of visa; Obtaining legal documentations from Israeli officials; Delivering presentations in Consular Department meetings; Preparing and examining passport applications and directing citizens to participate in relevant programs if qualified; Creating personalized profile, accompanying and supporting Israeli citizens throughout their applications, maintaining professional costumer-provider relationships; Testing new services in order to improve efficiency in the consular department; Assisting in planing and executing initiatives to reach the target audience through appropriate channels in order to engage them with relevant activities/special programs/ events offered for visitors/ citizens; Assisting in collaborating with professionals and Jewish organizations to coordinate awareness among the relevant community; Participating in collaboration with vendors to execute promotional Israeli/Jewish events and presenting advertising materials; promoting ideas and services,both individually and in community events, to support relationships with leaders/agencies in the Jewish community in Los Angeles .

Addendum

K. 9. Job 2 - Job Details

Ensuring VIP guests are satisfied with their stay; Coordinating between the different departments to meet vip guests' specific needs; Selling and distribution of membership card and loyalty program (priority club) to variety of clients attending the hotel; Maintaining and presenting promotional materials of the hotel offered services; Analyzing customer feedback and providing strategic direction to continuously improve overall rating, and delivering those presentations in meetings; Training new employees at the department; Identify potential guest in the hotel and offer/market exclusive and extended VIP services, as well as membership program; Creating and maintaining professional costumer-provider relationships with individuals or companies that use the hotel VIP and guest relations services; Maintaining professional relations with VIP clients during their stay and also thereafter throughout the year to ensure returning costumers; Ensuring special guests receive personalized services and establish relations with them; Promoting all hotel amenities, conveniences and programs offered; Directing and communicating programs to maintain perception of the hotel chain global services as well as distribution of the priority club membership and other local services.

Addendum

K. 9. Job 3 - Job Details

Presenting and arranging advertising materials for conferences, exhibitions and special events; Promoting services through media and commercial channels for clients; Coordinating all public relations activities and consulting with agents to produce campaigns; Organizing PR events to increase awareness of a company; Organizing and executing campaigns, as well as maintaining and updating promotional materials; Producing marketing materials, accessories, postal distribution, etc.; Conducting marketing tactics according to event type; Delivering reports and presentations on PR results.

EXHIBIT #4

Articles of Organization of a limited Liability Company

LLC-1	Articles of Organization of a Limited Liability Company (LLC)

201603910040

To form a limited liability company in California, you can fill out this form, and submit for filing along with:

- A **$70** filing fee.
- A separate, non-refundable **$15** service fee also must be included, if you drop off the completed form.

Important! LLCs in California may have to pay a minimum $800 yearly tax to the California Franchise Tax Board. For more information, go to https://www.ftb.ca.gov.

LLCs may not provide "professional services," as defined by California Corporations Code sections 13401(a) and 13401.3.

Note: *Before submitting the completed form*, you should consult with a private attorney for advice about your specific business needs.

FILED KB
Secretary of Sta
State of Californi
FEB 03 2016 mc

KPC This Space For Office Use Only

For questions about this form, go to *www.sos.ca.gov/business/be/filing-tips.htm.*

LLC Name (List the proposed LLC name exactly as it is to appear on the records of the California Secretary of State.)

① Consultants for America's Veterans, LLC

Proposed LLC Name

The name must include: LLC, L.L.C., Limited Liability Company, Limited Liability Co., Ltd. Liability Co. or Ltd. Liability Company; and may not include: bank, trust, trustee, incorporated, inc., corporation, or corp., insurer, or insurance company. For general entity name requirements and restrictions, go to www.sos.ca.gov/business/be/name-availability.htm.

Purpose

② The purpose of the limited liability company is to engage in any lawful act or activity for which a limited liability company may be organized under the California Revised Uniform Limited Liability Company Act.

LLC Addresses

③ a. [redacted] [redacted] [redacted]

Initial Street Address of Designated Office in CA - Do not list a P.O. Box | *City (no abbreviations)* | *State* | *Zip*

b. ____

Initial Mailing Address of LLC, if different from 3a | *City (no abbreviations)* | *State* | *Zip*

Service of Process (List a California resident or a California registered corporate agent that agrees to be your initial agent to accept service of process in case your LLC is sued. You may list any adult who lives in California. You may not list an LLC as the agent. Do not list an address if the agent is a California registered corporate agent as the address for service of process is already on file.)

④ a. LegalZoom.com, Inc.

Agent's Name

b. ____ CA

Agent's Street Address (if agent is not a corporation) - Do not list a P.O. Box | *City (no abbreviations)* | *State* | *Zip*

Management (Check only one.)

⑤ The LLC will be managed by:

☐ One Manager ☐ More Than One Manager ☑ All Limited Liability Company Member(s)

This form must be signed by each organizer. If you need more space, attach extra pages that are 1-sided and on standard letter-sized paper (8 1/2" x 11"). All attachments are made part of these articles of organization.

Organizer - Sign here By: [redacted]

Print your name here

Make check/money order payable to: **Secretary of State**	***By Mail***	***Drop-Off***
Upon filing, we will return one (1) uncertified copy of your filed document for free, and will certify the copy upon request and payment of a $5 certification fee.	Secretary of State Business Entities, P.O. Box 944228 Sacramento, CA 94244-2280	Secretary of State 1500 11th Street, 3rd Floor Sacramento, CA 95814

2014 California Secretary of State
www.sos.ca.gov/business/be

EXHIBIT #5

Operating Agreement

Operating Agreement

a California Limited Liability Company

THIS OPERATING AGREEMENT of Consultants for (the "Company") is entered into as of the date set forth on the signature page of this Agreement by each of the Members listed on Exhibit A of this Agreement.

A. The Members have formed the Company as a California limited liability company under the California Revised Uniform Limited Liability Company Act. The purpose of the Company is to conduct any lawful business for which limited liability companies may be organized under the laws of the state of California. The Members hereby adopt and approve the articles of organization of the Company filed with the California Secretary of State.

B. The Members enter into this Agreement to provide for the governance of the Company and the conduct of its business, and to specify their relative rights and obligations.

ARTICLE 1: DEFINITIONS

Capitalized terms used in this Agreement have the meanings specified in this Article 1 or elsewhere in this Agreement and if not so specified, have the meanings set forth in the California Revised Uniform Limited Liability Company Act.

"Agreement" means this Operating Agreement of the Company, as may be amended from time to time.

"Capital Account" means, with respect to any Member, an account consisting of such Member's Capital Contribution, (1) increased by such Member's allocated share of income and gain, (2) decreased by such Member's share of losses and deductions, (3) decreased by any distributions made by the Company to such Member, and (4) otherwise adjusted as required in accordance with applicable tax laws.

"Capital Contribution" means, with respect to any Member, the total value of (1) cash and the fair market value of property other than cash and (2) services that are contributed and/or agreed to be contributed to the Company by such Member, as listed on Exhibit A, as may be updated from time to time according to the terms of this Agreement.

"Exhibit" means a document attached to this Agreement labeled as "Exhibit A," "Exhibit B," and so forth, as such document may be amended, updated, or replaced from time to time according to the terms of this Agreement.

"Member" means each Person who acquires Membership Interest pursuant to this Agreement. The Members are listed on Exhibit A, as may be updated from time to time according to the terms of this Agreement. Each Member has the rights and obligations specified in this Agreement.

"Membership Interest" means the entire ownership interest of a Member in the Company at any particular time, including the right to any and all benefits to which a Member may be entitled as provided in this Agreement and under the California Revised Uniform Limited Liability Company Act, together with the obligations of the Member to comply with all of the terms and provisions of this Agreement.

"Ownership Interest" means the Percentage Interest or Units, as applicable, based on the manner in which relative ownership of the Company is divided.

"Percentage Interest" means the percentage of ownership in the Company that, with respect to each Member, entitles the Member to a Membership Interest and is expressed as either:

A. If ownership in the Company is expressed in terms of percentage, the percentage set forth opposite the name of each Member on Exhibit A, as may be adjusted from time to time pursuant to this Agreement; or

B. If ownership in the Company is expressed in Units, the ratio, expressed as a percentage, of:

(1) the number of Units owned by the Member (expressed as "MU" in the equation below) divided by

(2) the total number of Units owned by all of the Members of the Company (expressed as "TU" in the equation below).

$$\text{Percentage Interest} = \frac{MU}{TU}$$

"Person" means an individual (natural person), partnership, limited partnership, trust, estate, association, corporation, limited liability company, or other entity, whether domestic or foreign.

"Units" mean, if ownership in the Company is expressed in Units, units of ownership in the Company, that, with respect to each Member, entitles the Member to a Membership Interest which, if applicable, is expressed as the number of Units set forth opposite the name of each Member on Exhibit A, as may be adjusted from time to time pursuant to this Agreement.

ARTICLE 2: CAPITAL CONTRIBUTIONS, ADDITIONAL MEMBERS, CAPITAL ACCOUNTS AND LIMITED LIABILITY

2.1 **Initial Capital Contributions.** The names of all Members and each of their respective addresses, initial Capital Contributions, and Ownership Interests must be set forth on Exhibit A. Each Member has made or agrees to make the initial Capital Contribution set forth next to such Member's name on Exhibit A to become a Member of the Company.

2.2 **Subsequent Capital Contributions.** Members are not obligated to make additional Capital Contributions unless unanimously agreed by all the Members. If subsequent Capital Contributions are unanimously agreed by all the Members in a consent in writing, the Members may make such additional Capital Contributions on a pro rata basis in accordance with each Member's respective Percentage Interest or as otherwise unanimously agreed by the Members.

2.3 **Additional Members.**

A. With the exception of a transfer of interest (1) governed by Article 7 of this Agreement or (2) otherwise expressly authorized by this Agreement, additional Persons may become Members of the Company and be issued additional Ownership Interests only if approved by and on terms determined by a unanimous written agreement signed by all of the existing Members.

B. Before a Person may be admitted as a Member of the Company, that Person must sign and deliver to the Company the documents and instruments, in the form and containing the information required by the Company, that the Members deem necessary or desirable. Membership Interests of new Members will be allocated according to the terms of this Agreement.

2.4 **Capital Accounts.** Individual Capital Accounts must be maintained for each Member, unless (a) there is only one Member of the Company and (b) the Company is exempt according to applicable tax laws. Capital Accounts must be maintained in accordance with all applicable tax laws.

2.5 **Interest.** No interest will be paid by the Company or otherwise on Capital Contributions or on the balance of a Member's Capital Account.

2.6 **Limited Liability; No Authority.** A Member will not be bound by, or be personally liable for, the expenses, liabilities, debts, contracts, or obligations of the Company, except as otherwise provided in this Agreement or as required by the California Revised Uniform Limited Liability Company Act. Unless expressly provided in this Agreement, no Member, acting alone, has any authority to undertake or assume any obligation, debt, or responsibility, or otherwise act on behalf of, the Company or any other Member.

ARTICLE 3: ALLOCATIONS AND DISTRIBUTIONS

3.1 **Allocations.** Unless otherwise agreed to by the unanimous consent of the Members any income, gain, loss, deduction, or credit of the Company will be allocated for accounting and tax purposes on a pro rata basis in proportion to the respective Percentage Interest held by each Member and in compliance with applicable tax laws.

3.2 **Distributions.** The Company will have the right to make distributions of cash and property to the Members on a pro rata basis in proportion to the respective Percentage Interest held by each Member. The timing and amount of distributions will be determined by the Members in accordance with the California Revised Uniform Limited Liability Company Act.

3.3 **Limitations on Distributions.** The Company must not make a distribution to a Member if, after giving effect to the distribution:

A. The Company would be unable to pay its debts as they become due in the usual course of business; or

B. The fair value of the Company's total assets would be less than the sum of its total liabilities plus the amount that would be needed, if the Company were to be dissolved at the time of the distribution, to satisfy the preferential rights upon dissolution of Members, if any, whose preferential rights are superior to those of the Members receiving the distribution.

ARTICLE 4: MANAGEMENT

4.1 **Management.**

A. **Generally.** Subject to the terms of this Agreement and the California Revised Uniform Limited Liability Company Act, the business and affairs of the Company will be managed by the Members.

B. **Approval and Action.** Unless greater or other authorization is required pursuant to this Agreement or under the California Revised Uniform Limited Liability Company Act for the Company to engage in an activity or transaction, all activities or transactions must be approved by the Members, to constitute the act of the Company or serve to bind the Company. With such approval, the signature of any Members authorized to sign on behalf of the Company is sufficient to bind the Company with respect to the matter or matters so approved. Without such approval, no Members acting alone may bind the Company to any agreement with or obligation to any third party or represent or claim to have the ability to so bind the Company.

C. **Certain Decisions Requiring Greater Authorization.** Notwithstanding clause B above, the following matters require unanimous approval of the Members in a consent in writing to constitute an act of the Company:

(i) A material change in the purposes or the nature of the Company's business;

(ii) With the exception of a transfer of interest governed by Article 7 of this Agreement, the admission of a new Member or a change in any Member's Membership Interest, Ownership Interest, Percentage Interest, or Voting Interest in any manner other than in accordance with this Agreement;

(iii) The merger of the Company with any other entity or the sale of all or substantially all of the Company's assets; and

(iv) The amendment of this Agreement.

4.2 **Officers.** The Members are authorized to appoint one or more officers from time to time. The officers will have the titles, the authority, exercise the powers, and perform the duties that the Members determine from time to time. Each officer will continue to perform and hold office until such time as (a) the officer's successor is chosen and appointed by the Members; or (b) the officer is dismissed or terminated by the Members, which termination will be subject to applicable law and, if an effective employment agreement exists between the officer and the Company, the employment agreement. Subject to applicable law and the employment agreement (if any), each officer will serve at the direction of Members, and may be terminated, at any time and for any reason, by the Members.

ARTICLE 5: ACCOUNTS AND ACCOUNTING

5.1 **Accounts.** The Company must maintain complete accounting records of the Company's business, including a full and accurate record of each Company transaction. The records must be kept at the Company's principal executive office and must be open to inspection and copying by Members during normal business hours upon reasonable notice by the Members wishing to inspect or copy the records or their authorized representatives, for purposes reasonably related to the Membership Interest of such Members. The costs of inspection and copying will be borne by the respective Member.

5.2 **Records.** The Members will keep or cause the Company to keep the following business records.

(i) An up to date list of the Members, each of their respective full legal names, last known business or residence address, Capital Contributions, the amount and terms of any agreed upon future Capital Contributions, and Ownership Interests, and Voting Interests;

(ii) A copy of the Company's federal, state, and local tax information and income tax returns and reports, if any, for the six most recent taxable years;

(iii) A copy of the articles of organization of the Company, as may be amended from time to time ("Articles of Organization"); and

(iv) An original signed copy, which may include counterpart signatures, of this Agreement, and any amendments to this Agreement, signed by all then-current Members.

5.3 **Income Tax Returns.** Within 45 days after the end of each taxable year, the Company will use its best efforts to send each of the Members all information necessary for the Members to complete their federal and state tax information, returns, and reports and a copy of the Company's federal, state, and local tax information or income tax returns and reports for such year.

5.4 **Subchapter S Election.** The Company may, upon unanimous consent of the Members, elect to be treated for income tax purposes as an S Corporation. This designation may be changed as permitted under the Internal Revenue Code Section 1362(d) and applicable Regulations.

5.5 **Tax Matters Member.** Anytime the Company is required to designate or select a tax matters partner pursuant to Section 6231(a)(7) of the Internal Revenue Code and any regulations issued by the Internal Revenue Service, the Members must designate one of the Members as the tax matters partner of the Company and keep such designation in effect at all times.

5.6 **Banking.** All funds of the Company must be deposited in one or more bank accounts in the name of the Company with one or more recognized financial institutions. The Members are authorized to establish such accounts and complete, sign, and deliver any banking resolutions reasonably required by the respective financial institutions in order to establish an account.

ARTICLE 6: MEMBERSHIP – VOTING AND MEETINGS

6.1 **Members and Voting Rights.** The Members have the right and power to vote on all matters with respect to which the Articles of Organization, this Agreement, or the California Revised Uniform Limited Liability Company Act requires or permits. Unless otherwise stated in this Agreement (for example, in Section 4.1(c)) or required under the California Revised Uniform Limited Liability Company Act, the vote of the Members holding at least a majority of the Voting Interest of the Company is required to approve or carry out an action.

6.2 **Meetings of Members.** Annual, regular, or special meetings of the Members are not required but may be held at such time and place as the Members deem necessary or desirable for the reasonable management of the Company. Meetings may be called by any Member or Members, holding 10% or more of the Percentage Interests, for the purpose of addressing any matters on which the Members may vote. A written notice setting forth the date, time, and location of a meeting must be sent at least ten (10) days but no more than sixty (60) days before the date of the meeting to each Member entitled to vote at the meeting. A Member may waive notice of a meeting by sending a signed waiver to the Company's principal executive office or as otherwise provided in the California Revised Uniform Limited Liability Company Act. In any instance in which the approval of the Members is required under this Agreement, such approval may be obtained in any manner permitted by the California Revised Uniform Limited Liability Company Act, including by conference call or similar communications equipment. Any action that could be taken at a meeting may be approved by a consent in writing that describes the action to be taken and is signed by Members holding the minimum Voting Interest required to approve the action. If any action is taken without a meeting and without unanimous written consent of the Members, notice of such action must be sent to each Member that did not consent to the action.

ARTICLE 7: WITHDRAWAL AND TRANSFERS OF MEMBERSHIP INTERESTS

7.1 **Withdrawal.** Members may withdraw from the Company prior to the dissolution and winding up of the Company (a) by transferring or assigning all of their respective Membership Interests pursuant to Section 7.2 below, or (b) if all of the Members unanimously agree in a written consent. Subject to the provisions of Article 3, a Member that withdraws pursuant to this Section 7.1 will be entitled to a distribution from the Company in an amount equal to such Member's Capital Account, which must be paid by the Company to such Member within ninety (90) days of the withdrawal date unless otherwise agreed in writing.

7.2 **Restrictions on Transfer; Admission of Transferee.** A Member may transfer Membership Interests to any other Person without the consent of any other Member. A person may acquire Membership Interests directly from the Company upon the written consent of all Members. A Person that acquires Membership Interests in accordance with this Section 7.2 will be admitted as a Member of the Company only after the requirements of Section 2.3(b) are complied with in full.

ARTICLE 8: DISSOLUTION

8.1 **Dissolution.** The Company will be dissolved upon the first to occur of the following events:

(i) The vote of the Members holding at least a majority of the Voting Interest of the Company to dissolve the Company;

(ii) Entry of a decree of judicial dissolution under Section 17707.01 of the California Revised Uniform Limited Liability Company Act;

(iii) The sale or transfer of all or substantially all of the Company's assets;

(iv) A merger or consolidation of the Company with one or more entities in which the Company is not the surviving entity; or

(v) The Company has no members during 90 consecutive days, except on the death of a natural person who is the sole member of the Company, the status of the member, including Membership Interest, may pass to the heirs, successors, and assigns of the member by will or applicable law.

8.2 **No Automatic Dissolution Upon Certain Events.** Unless otherwise set forth in this Agreement or required by applicable law, the death, incapacity, disassociation, bankruptcy, or withdrawal of a Member will not automatically cause a dissolution of the Company.

ARTICLE 9: INDEMNIFICATION

9.1 **Indemnification.** The Company has the power to defend, indemnify, and hold harmless any Person who was or is a party, or who is threatened to be made a party, to any Proceeding (as that term is defined below) by reason of the fact that such Person was or is a Member, officer, employee, representative, or other agent of the Company, or was or is serving at the request of the Company as a director, Governor, officer, employee, representative or other agent of another limited liability company, corporation, partnership, joint venture, trust, or other enterprise (each such Person is referred to as a "Company Agent"), against Expenses (as that term is defined below), judgments, fines, settlements, and other amounts (collectively, "Damages") to the maximum extent now or hereafter permitted under California law. "Proceeding," as used in this Article 9, means any threatened, pending, or completed action, proceeding, individual claim or matter within a proceeding, whether civil, criminal, administrative, or investigative. "Expenses," as used in this Article 9, includes, without limitation, court costs, reasonable attorney and expert fees, and any expenses incurred relating to establishing a right to indemnification, if any, under this Article 9.

9.2 **Mandatory.** The Company must defend, indemnify and hold harmless a Company Agent in connection with a Proceeding in which such Company Agent is involved if, and to the extent, California law requires that a limited liability company indemnify a Company Agent in connection with a Proceeding.

9.3 **Expenses Paid by the Company Prior to Final Disposition.** Expenses of each Company Agent indemnified or held harmless under this Agreement that are actually and reasonably incurred in connection with the defense or settlement of a Proceeding may be paid by the Company in advance of the final disposition of a Proceeding if authorized by a vote of the Members that are not seeking indemnification holding a majority of the Voting Interests (excluding the Voting Interest of the Company Agent seeking indemnification). Before the Company makes any such payment of Expenses, the Company Agent seeking indemnification must deliver a written undertaking to the Company stating that such Company Agent will repay the applicable Expenses to the Company unless it is ultimately determined that the Company Agent is entitled or required to be indemnified and held harmless by the Company (as set forth in Sections 9.1 or 9.2 above or as otherwise required by applicable law).

ARTICLE 10: GENERAL PROVISIONS

10.1 **Notice.** (a) Any notices (including requests, demands, or other communications) to be sent by one party to another party in connection with this Agreement must be in writing and delivered personally, by reputable overnight courier, or by certified mail (or equivalent service offered by the postal service from time to time) to the following addresses or as otherwise notified in accordance with this Section: (i) if to the Company, notices must be sent to the Company's principal executive office; and (ii) if to a Member, notices must be sent to the Member's last known address for notice on record. (b) Any party to this Agreement may change its notice address by sending written notice of such change to the Company in the manner specified above. Notice will be deemed to have been duly given as follows: (i) upon delivery, if delivered personally or by reputable overnight carrier or (ii) five days after the date of posting if sent by certified mail.

10.2 **Entire Agreement; Amendment.** This Agreement along with the Articles of Organization (together, the "Organizational Documents"), constitute the entire agreement among the Members and replace and supersede all prior written and oral understandings and agreements with respect to the subject matter of this Agreement, except as otherwise required by the California Revised Uniform Limited Liability Company Act. There are no representations, agreements, arrangements, or undertakings, oral or written, between or among the Members relating to the subject matter of this Agreement that are not fully expressed in the Organizational Documents. This Agreement may not be modified or amended in any respect, except in a writing signed by all of the Members, except as otherwise required or permitted by the California Revised Uniform Limited Liability Company Act.

10.3 **Governing Law; Severability.** This Agreement will be construed and enforced in accordance with the laws of the state of California. If any provision of this Agreement is held to be unenforceable by a court of competent jurisdiction for any reason whatsoever, (i) the validity, legality, and enforceability of the remaining provisions of this Agreement (including without limitation, all portions of any provisions containing any such unenforceable provision that are not themselves unenforceable) will not in any way be affected or impaired thereby, and (ii) to the fullest extent possible, the unenforceable provision will be deemed modified and replaced by a provision that approximates the intent and economic effect of the unenforceable provision and the Agreement will be deemed amended accordingly.

10.4 **Further Action.** Each Member agrees to perform all further acts and execute, acknowledge, and deliver any documents which may be reasonably necessary, appropriate, or desirable to carry out the provisions of this Agreement.

10.5 **No Third Party Beneficiary.** This Agreement is made solely for the benefit of the parties to this Agreement and their respective permitted successors and assigns, and no other Person or entity will have or acquire any right by virtue of this Agreement. This Agreement will be binding on and inure to the benefit of the parties and their heirs, personal representatives, and permitted successors and assigns.

10.6 **Incorporation by Reference.** The recitals and each appendix, exhibit, schedule, and other document attached to or referred to in this Agreement are hereby incorporated into this Agreement by reference.

10.7 **Counterparts.** This Agreement may be executed in any number of counterparts with the same effect as if all of the Members signed the same copy. All counterparts will be construed together and will constitute one agreement.

[Remainder Intentionally Left Blank.]

IN WITNESS WHEREOF, the parties have executed or caused to be executed this Operating Agreement and do each hereby represent and warrant that their respective signatory, whose signature appears below, has been and is, on the date of this Agreement, duly authorized to execute this Agreement.

Dated: 12/13/2016

EXHIBIT #6

Members

<u>EXHIBIT A</u>
MEMBERS

The Members of the Company and their respective addresses, Capital Contributions, and Ownership Interests are set forth below. The Members agree to keep this Exhibit A current and updated in accordance with the terms of this Agreement, including, but not limited to, Sections 2.1, 2.3, 2.4, 7.1, 7.2, and 10.1.

Members	**Capital Contribution**	**Percentage Interest**
[redacted] Address: [redacted] San Diego, California 92123		100%

EXHIBIT 7

Officers

EXHIBIT B
OFFICERS

Officers of the Company are set forth below.

Name of Officer	Title
Chief Information Officer	
Chief Financial Officer	
President	
Chief Executive Officer	

<u>EXHIBIT #8</u>

IRS Letter

IRS DEPARTMENT OF THE TREASURY
INTERNAL REVENUE SERVICE
CINCINNATI OH 45999-0023

Date of this notice: 02-11-2016

Employer Identification Number:
81-1415824

Form: SS-4

Number of this notice: CP 575 B

For assistance you may call us at:
1-800-829-4933

IF YOU WRITE, ATTACH THE
STUB AT THE END OF THIS NOTICE.

CONSULTANTS
LLC
CAV
%
SAN DIEGO, CA 92123

WE ASSIGNED YOU AN EMPLOYER IDENTIFICATION NUMBER

Thank you for applying for an Employer Identification Number (EIN). We assigned you This EIN will identify you, your business accounts, tax returns, and documents, even if you have no employees. Please keep this notice in your permanent records.

When filing tax documents, payments, and related correspondence, it is very important that you use your EIN and complete name and address exactly as shown above. Any variation may cause a delay in processing, result in incorrect information in your account, or even cause you to be assigned more than one EIN. If the information is not correct as shown above, please make the correction using the attached tear off stub and return it to us.

Based on the information received from you or your representative, you must file the following form(s) by the date(s) shown.

Form 1065	04/15/2017

If you have questions about the form(s) or the due date(s) shown, you can call us at the phone number or write to us at the address shown at the top of this notice. If you need help in determining your annual accounting period (tax year), see Publication 538, *Accounting Periods and Methods.*

We assigned you a tax classification based on information obtained from you or your representative. It is not a legal determination of your tax classification, and is not binding on the IRS. If you want a legal determination of your tax classification, you may request a private letter ruling from the IRS under the guidelines in Revenue Procedure 2004-1, 2004-1 I.R.B. 1 (or superseding Revenue Procedure for the year at issue). Note: Certain tax classification elections can be requested by filing Form 8832, *Entity Classification Election.* See Form 8832 and its instructions for additional information.

A limited liability company (LLC) may file Form 8832, *Entity Classification Election*, and elect to be classified as an association taxable as a corporation. If the LLC is eligible to be treated as a corporation that meets certain tests and it will be electing S corporation status, it must timely file Form 2553, *Election by a Small Business Corporation.* The LLC will be treated as a corporation as of the effective date of the S corporation election and does not need to file Form 8832.

To obtain tax forms and publications, including those referenced in this notice, visit our Web site at www.irs.gov. If you do not have access to the Internet, call 1-800-829-3676 (TTY/TDD 1-800-829-4059) or visit your local IRS office.

(IRS USE ONLY)   575B   02-11-2016 CONS B 9999999999 SS-4

IMPORTANT REMINDERS:

* Keep a copy of this notice in your permanent records. **This notice is issued only one time and the IRS will not be able to generate a duplicate copy for you.** You may give a copy of this document to anyone asking for proof of your EIN.

* Use this EIN and your name exactly as they appear at the top of this notice on all your federal tax forms.

* Refer to this EIN on your tax-related correspondence and documents.

If you have questions about your EIN, you can call us at the phone number or write to us at the address shown at the top of this notice. If you write, please tear off the stub at the bottom of this notice and send it along with your letter. If you do not need to write us, do not complete and return the stub.

Your name control associated with this EIN is CONS. You will need to provide this information, along with your EIN, if you file your returns electronically.

Thank you for your cooperation.

Keep this part for your records.   CP 575 B (Rev. 7-2007)

Return this part with any correspondence so we may identify your account. Please correct any errors in your name or address.

CP 575 B

9999999999

Your Telephone Number Best Time to Call
(   )   -

DATE OF THIS NOTICE: 02-11-2016
EMPLOYER IDENTIFICATION NUMBER:
FORM: SS-4   NOBOD

INTERNAL REVENUE SERVICE
CINCINNATI OH 45999-0023

CONSULTANTS
LLC
CAV
% RUDY SAMUEL MELSON MBR

EXHIBIT #9

Applicant's 2016 Federal Tax Return

Form **1040** Department of the Treasury—Internal Revenue Service (99)
U.S. Individual Income Tax Return **2016** OMB No. 1545-0074 IRS Use Only—Do not write or staple in this space.

For the year Jan. 1–Dec. 31, 2016, or other tax year beginning , 2016, ending , 20 See separate instructions.

Your first name and initial	Last name	Your social security number
[redacted]	[redacted]	[redacted]
If a joint return, spouse's first name and initial	Last name	Spouse's social security number
Home address (number and street). If you have a P.O. box, see instructions. [redacted]	Apt. no. 10103	Make sure the SSN(s) above and on line 6c are correct.
City, town or post office, state, and ZIP code. If you have a foreign address, also complete spaces below (see instructions). [redacted] CA 92123		Presidential Election Campaign: Check here if you, or your spouse if filing jointly, want $3 to go to this fund. Checking a box below will not change your tax or refund. ☐ You ☐ Spouse
Foreign country name	Foreign province/state/county	Foreign postal code

Filing Status

Check only one box.

1 [X] Single
2 [ ] Married filing jointly (even if only one had income)
3 [ ] Married filing separately. Enter spouse's SSN above and full name here. ▶
4 [ ] Head of household (with qualifying person). (See instructions.) If the qualifying person is a child but not your dependent, enter this child's name here. ▶
5 [ ] Qualifying widow(er) with dependent child

Exemptions

6a [X] **Yourself.** If someone can claim you as a dependent, do not check box 6a
b [ ] **Spouse**

Boxes checked on 6a and 6b: 1

c **Dependents:**

(1) First name Last name	(2) Dependent's social security number	(3) Dependent's relationship to you	(4) ✓ if child under age 17 qualifying for child tax credit (see instr.)
[redacted]	[redacted]	OTHER	☐
			☐
			☐
			☐

If more than four dependents, see instructions and check here ▶ ☐

No. of children on 6c who:
- lived with you
- did not live with you due to divorce or separation (see instructions)

Dependents on 6c not entered above: 1

d Total number of exemptions claimed — Add numbers on lines above ▶ 2

Income

Attach Form(s) W-2 here. Also attach Forms W-2G and 1099-R if tax was withheld.

If you did not get a W-2, see instructions.

Line	Description		Line	Amount
7	Wages, salaries, tips, etc. Attach Form(s) W-2		7	48,311
8a	**Taxable** interest. Attach Schedule B if required		8a	
b	**Tax-exempt** interest. **Do not** include on line 8a	8b		
9a	Ordinary dividends. Attach Schedule B if required		9a	
b	Qualified dividends	9b		
10	Taxable refunds, credits, or offsets of state and local income taxes		10	
11	Alimony received		11	
12	Business income or (loss). Attach Schedule C or C-EZ		12	70,083
13	Capital gain or (loss). Attach Schedule D if required. If not required, check here ▶ ☐		13	
14	Other gains or (losses). Attach Form 4797		14	
15a	IRA distributions 15a	b Taxable amount	15b	
16a	Pensions and annuities 16a	b Taxable amount	16b	
17	Rental real estate, royalties, partnerships, S corporations, trusts, etc. Attach Schedule E		17	
18	Farm income or (loss). Attach Schedule F		18	
19	Unemployment compensation		19	
20a	Social security benefits 20a	b Taxable amount	20b	
21	Other income. List type and amount TOTAL DEBT CANCELED		21	14,487
22	Combine the amounts in the far right column for lines 7 through 21. This is your **total income** ▶		22	132,881

Adjusted Gross Income

Line	Description	Line	Amount	Line	Amount
23	Educator expenses	23			
24	Certain business expenses of reservists, performing artists, and fee-basis government officials. Attach Form 2106 or 2106-EZ	24			
25	Health savings account deduction. Attach Form 8889	25			
26	Moving expenses. Attach Form 3903	26			
27	Deductible part of self-employment tax. Attach Schedule SE	27	4,951		
28	Self-employed SEP, SIMPLE, and qualified plans	28			
29	Self-employed health insurance deduction	29			
30	Penalty on early withdrawal of savings	30			
31a	Alimony paid b Recipient's SSN ▶	31a			
32	IRA deduction	32			
33	Student loan interest deduction	33			
34	Tuition and fees. Attach Form 8917	34			
35	Domestic production activities deduction. Attach Form 8903	35			
36	Add lines 23 through 35			36	4,951
37	Subtract line 36 from line 22. This is your **adjusted gross income** ▶			37	127,930

	38	Amount from line 37 (adjusted gross income)	38	127,930
Tax and Credits	39a	Check if: ☐ You were born before January 2, 1952, ☐ Blind. ☐ Spouse was born before January 2, 1952, ☐ Blind. Total boxes checked ▶ 39a ☐		
	b	If your spouse itemizes on a separate return or you were a dual-status alien, check here ▶ 39b ☐		
Standard Deduction for—	40	Itemized deductions (from Schedule A) or your standard deduction (see left margin)	40	6,300
	41	Subtract line 40 from line 38	41	121,630
• People who check any box on line 39a or 39b or who can be claimed as a dependent, see instructions.	42	Exemptions. If line 38 is $155,650 or less, multiply $4,050 by the number on line 6d. Otherwise, see instructions	42	8,100
	43	Taxable income. Subtract line 42 from line 41. If line 42 is more than line 41, enter -0-	43	113,530
	44	Tax (see instr.) Check if any from: a ☐ Form(s) 8814 b ☐ Form 4972 c ☐	44	24,825
	45	Alternative minimum tax (see instructions). Attach Form 6251	45	
	46	Excess advance premium tax credit repayment. Attach Form 8962	46	
• All others:	47	Add lines 44, 45, and 46 ▶	47	24,825
Single or Married filing separately, $6,300	48	Foreign tax credit. Attach Form 1116 if required	48	
	49	Credit for child and dependent care expenses. Attach Form 2441	49	
	50	Education credits from Form 8863, line 19	50	
Married filing jointly or Qualifying widow(er), $12,600	51	Retirement savings contributions credit. Attach Form 8880	51	
	52	Child tax credit. Attach Schedule 8812, if required	52	
	53	Residential energy credits. Attach Form 5695	53	
Head of household, $9,300	54	Other credits from Form: a ☐ 3800 b ☐ 8801 c ☐	54	
	55	Add lines 48 through 54. These are your total credits	55	
	56	Subtract line 55 from line 47. If line 55 is more than line 47, enter -0- ▶	56	24,825
Other Taxes	57	Self-employment tax. Attach Schedule SE	57	9,902
	58	Unreported social security and Medicare tax from Form: a ☐ 4137 b ☐ 8919	58	
	59	Additional tax on IRAs, other qualified retirement plans, etc. Attach Form 5329 if required	59	
	60a	Household employment taxes from Schedule H	60a	
	b	First-time homebuyer credit repayment. Attach Form 5405 if required	60b	
	61	Health care: individual responsibility (see instructions) Full-year coverage [X]	61	
	62	Taxes from: a ☐ Form 8959 b ☐ Form 8960 c ☐ Instructions; enter code(s)	62	
	63	Add lines 56 through 62. This is your total tax ▶	63	34,727
Payments	64	Federal income tax withheld from Forms W-2 and 1099	64	7,924
	65	2016 estimated tax payments and amount applied from 2015 return	65	
If you have a qualifying child, attach Schedule EIC.	66a	Earned income credit (EIC)	66a	
	b	Nontaxable combat pay election 66b		
	67	Additional child tax credit. Attach Schedule 8812	67	
	68	American opportunity credit from Form 8863, line 8	68	
	69	Net premium tax credit. Attach Form 8962	69	
	70	Amount paid with request for extension to file	70	
	71	Excess social security and tier 1 RRTA tax withheld	71	
	72	Credit for federal tax on fuels. Attach Form 4136	72	
	73	Credits from Form: a ☐ 2439 b ☐ Reserved c ☐ 8885 d ☐	73	
	74	Add lines 64, 65, 66a, and 67 through 73. These are your total payments ▶	74	7,924
Refund	75	If line 74 is more than line 63, subtract line 63 from line 74. This is the amount you overpaid	75	
	76a	Amount of line 75 you want refunded to you. If Form 8888 is attached, check here ▶ ☐	76a	
Direct deposit? See instructions.	▶ b	Routing number ▶ c Type: ☐ Checking ☐ Savings		
	▶ d	Account number		
	77	Amount of line 75 you want applied to your 2017 estimated tax ▶ 77		
Amount You Owe	78	Amount you owe. Subtract line 74 from line 63. For details on how to pay, see instructions ▶	78	26,959
	79	Estimated tax penalty (see instructions) 79: 156		

Third Party Designee

Do you want to allow another person to discuss this return with the IRS (see instructions)? [X] Yes. Complete below. ☐ No

Designee's name ▶ [redacted] Phone no. ▶ [redacted] Personal identification number (PIN) ▶ 48059

Sign Here

Under penalties of perjury, I declare that I have examined this return and accompanying schedules and statements, and to the best of my knowledge and belief, they are true, correct, and accurately list all amounts and sources of income I received during the tax year. Declaration of preparer (other than taxpayer) is based on all information of which preparer has any knowledge.

Joint return? See instr. Keep a copy for your records.

Your signature	Date	Your occupation	Daytime phone number
		PROFESSOR	
Spouse's signature. If a joint return, both must sign.	Date	Spouse's occupation	If the IRS sent you an Identity Protection PIN, enter it here (see instr.)

Paid Preparer Use Only

Print/Type preparer's name	Preparer's signature	Date	Check ☐ if self-employed	PTIN
LEON BORODA	LEON BORODA	03/14/17		[redacted]

Firm's name ▶ [redacted] Firm's EIN ▶ [redacted]

Firm's address ▶ [redacted] Phone no. [redacted]

SCHEDULE C (Form 1040)

Department of the Treasury Internal Revenue Service (99)

Profit or Loss From Business

(Sole Proprietorship)

▶ Information about Schedule C and its separate instructions is at *www.irs.gov/schedulec*.
▶ Attach to Form 1040, 1040NR, or 1041; partnerships generally must file Form 1065.

OMB No. 1545-0074

2016

Attachment Sequence No. 09

Name of proprietor: [redacted] | Social security number (SSN): [redacted]

A Principal business or profession, including product or service (see instructions): [redacted]

B Enter code from instructions ▶ 999999

C Business name. If no separate business name, leave blank. [redacted]

D Employer ID number (EIN), (see instr.)

E Business address (including suite or room no.) ▶ [redacted]
City, town or post office, state, and ZIP code [redacted]

F Accounting method: (1) [X] Cash (2) [ ] Accrual (3) [ ] Other (specify) ▶

G Did you "materially participate" in the operation of this business during 2016? If "No," see instructions for limit on losses — [X] Yes [ ] No

H If you started or acquired this business during 2016, check here ▶ [ ]

I Did you make any payments in 2016 that would require you to file Form(s) 1099? (see instructions) — [ ] Yes [X] No

J If "Yes," did you or will you file required Forms 1099? — [ ] Yes [ ] No

Part I Income

		Line	Amount
1	Gross receipts or sales. See instructions for line 1 and check the box if this income was reported to you on Form W-2 and the "Statutory employee" box on that form was checked ▶ [ ]	1	121,236
2	Returns and allowances	2	
3	Subtract line 2 from line 1	3	121,236
4	Cost of goods sold (from line 42)	4	
5	**Gross profit.** Subtract line 4 from line 3	5	121,236
6	Other income, including federal and state gasoline or fuel tax credit or refund (see instructions)	6	
7	**Gross income.** Add lines 5 and 6 ▶	7	121,236

Part II Expenses. Enter expenses for business use of your home only on line 30.

		Line	Amount			Line	Amount
8	Advertising	8		18	Office expense (see instructions)	18	2,691
9	Car and truck expenses (see instructions)	9	5,157	19	Pension and profit-sharing plans	19	
				20	Rent or lease (see instructions):		
10	Commissions and fees	10		a	Vehicles, machinery, and equipment	20a	7,714
11	Contract labor (see instructions)	11		b	Other business property	20b	15,416
12	Depletion	12		21	Repairs and maintenance	21	
13	Depreciation and section 179 expense deduction (not included in Part III) (see instructions)	13		22	Supplies (not included in Part III)	22	1,000
				23	Taxes and licenses	23	
				24	Travel, meals, and entertainment:		
14	Employee benefit programs (other than on line 19)	14		a	Travel	24a	12,325
				b	Deductible meals and entertainment (see instructions)	24b	
15	Insurance (other than health)	15	206	25	Utilities	25	
16	Interest:						
a	Mortgage (paid to banks, etc.)	16a		26	Wages (less employment credits)	26	
b	Other	16b		27a	Other expenses (from line 48)	27a	1,894
17	Legal and professional services	17	4,750	b	Reserved for future use	27b	

		Line	Amount
28	**Total expenses** before expenses for business use of home. Add lines 8 through 27a ▶	28	51,153
29	Tentative profit or (loss). Subtract line 28 from line 7	29	70,083
30	Expenses for business use of your home. Do not report these expenses elsewhere. Attach Form 8829 unless using the simplified method (see instructions). **Simplified method filers only:** enter the total square footage of: (a) your home: ______ and (b) the part of your home used for business: ______ . Use the Simplified Method Worksheet in the instructions to figure the amount to enter on line 30	30	
31	**Net profit or (loss).** Subtract line 30 from line 29. • If a profit, enter on both **Form 1040, line 12** (or **Form 1040NR, line 13**) and on **Schedule SE, line 2.** (If you checked the box on line 1, see instructions). Estates and trusts, enter on **Form 1041, line 3.** • If a loss, you **must** go to line 32.	31	70,083
32	If you have a loss, check the box that describes your investment in this activity (see instructions). • If you checked 32a, enter the loss on both **Form 1040, line 12,** (or **Form 1040NR, line 13**) and on **Schedule SE, line 2.** (If you checked the box on line 1, see the line 31 instructions). Estates and trusts, enter on **Form 1041, line 3.** • If you checked 32b, you **must** attach **Form 6198.** Your loss may be limited.	32a [ ] All investment is at risk. 32b [ ] Some investment is not at risk.	

For Paperwork Reduction Act Notice, see the separate instructions.
DAA

Part III Cost of Goods Sold (see instructions)

33 Method(s) used to value closing inventory: a ☐ Cost b ☐ Lower of cost or market c ☐ Other (attach explanation)

34 Was there any change in determining quantities, costs, or valuations between opening and closing inventory? If "Yes," attach explanation ☐ Yes ☐ No

35	Inventory at beginning of year. If different from last year's closing inventory, attach explanation	35	
36	Purchases less cost of items withdrawn for personal use	36	
37	Cost of labor. Do not include any amounts paid to yourself	37	
38	Materials and supplies	38	
39	Other costs	39	
40	Add lines 35 through 39	40	
41	Inventory at end of year	41	
42	**Cost of goods sold.** Subtract line 41 from line 40. Enter the result here and on line 4	42	

Part IV Information on Your Vehicle. Complete this part **only** if you are claiming car or truck expenses on line 9 and are not required to file Form 4562 for this business. See the instructions for line 13 to find out if you must file Form 4562.

43 When did you place your vehicle in service for business purposes? (month, day, year) ▶ 01/01/15

44 Of the total number of miles you drove your vehicle during 2016, enter the number of miles you used your vehicle for:

a Business 8,000 b Commuting (see instructions) c Other 2,000

45 Was your vehicle available for personal use during off-duty hours? ☒ Yes ☐ No

46 Do you (or your spouse) have another vehicle available for personal use? ☒ Yes ☐ No

47a Do you have evidence to support your deduction? ☐ Yes ☒ No

b If "Yes," is the evidence written? ☐ Yes ☐ No

Part V Other Expenses. List below business expenses not included on lines 8-26 or line 30.

BUSINESS CELL PHONE	1,190
OFFICE TELEPHONE	420
EFAX	284

48 **Total other expenses.** Enter here and on line 27a | 48 | 1,894

SCHEDULE SE (Form 1040) Department of the Treasury Internal Revenue Service (99)	**Self-Employment Tax** ▶ Information about Schedule SE and its separate instructions is at *www.irs.gov/schedulese.* ▶ Attach to Form 1040 or Form 1040NR.	OMB No. 1545-0074 **2016** Attachment Sequence No. **17**

Name of person with **self-employment** income (as shown on Form 1040 or Form 1040NR)	Social security number of person with **self-employment** income ▶	102-76-6029

Before you begin: To determine if you must file Schedule SE, see the instructions.

May I Use Short Schedule SE or Must I Use Long Schedule SE?

Note. Use this flowchart **only** if you must file Schedule SE. If unsure, see *Who Must File Schedule SE* in the instructions.

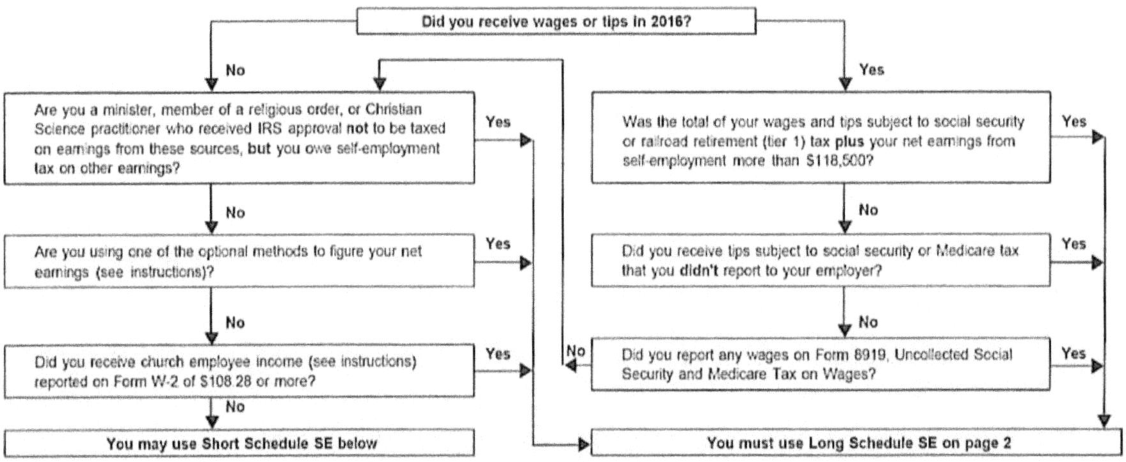

Section A — Short Schedule SE. Caution. Read above to see if you can use Short Schedule SE.

1a	Net farm profit or (loss) from Schedule F, line 34, and farm partnerships, Schedule K-1 (Form 1065), box 14, code A	1a	
b	If you received social security retirement or disability benefits, enter the amount of Conservation Reserve Program payments included on Schedule F, line 4b, or listed on Schedule K-1 (Form 1065), box 20, code Z	1b	( )
2	Net profit or (loss) from Schedule C, line 31; Schedule C-EZ, line 3; Schedule K-1 (Form 1065), box 14, code A (other than farming); and Schedule K-1 (Form 1065-B), box 9, code J1. Ministers and members of religious orders, see instructions for types of income to report on this line. See instructions for other income to report	2	70,083
3	Combine lines 1a, 1b, and 2	3	70,083
4	Multiply line 3 by 92.35% (0.9235). If less than $400, you don't owe self-employment tax; **don't** file this schedule unless you have an amount on line 1b ▶ **Note.** If line 4 is less than $400 due to Conservation Reserve Program payments on line 1b, see instructions.	4	64,722
5	**Self-employment tax.** If the amount on line 4 is: • $118,500 or less, multiply line 4 by 15.3% (0.153). Enter the result here and on **Form 1040, line 57,** or **Form 1040NR, line 55** • More than $118,500, multiply line 4 by 2.9% (0.029). Then, add $14,694 to the result. Enter the total here and on **Form 1040, line 57,** or **Form 1040NR, line 55**	5	9,902
6	**Deduction for one-half of self-employment tax.** Multiply line 5 by 50% (0.50). Enter the result here and on **Form 1040, line 27,** or **Form 1040NR, line 27** — 6: 4,951		

For Paperwork Reduction Act Notice, see your tax return instructions. **Schedule SE (Form 1040) 2016**

DAA

Form **6251** Department of the Treasury Internal Revenue Service (99)

Alternative Minimum Tax—Individuals

▶ Information about Form 6251 and its separate instructions is at *www.irs.gov/form6251.*

▶ Attach to Form 1040 or Form 1040NR.

OMB No. 1545-0074

2016

Attachment Sequence No. 32

Name(s) shown on Form 1040 or Form 1040NR: [redacted]

Your social security number: [redacted]

Part I Alternative Minimum Taxable Income (See instructions for how to complete each line.)

Line	Description	No.	Amount
1	If filing Schedule A (Form 1040), enter the amount from Form 1040, line 41, and go to line 2. Otherwise, enter the amount from Form 1040, line 38, and go to line 7. (If less than zero, enter as a negative amount.)	1	127,930
2	Medical and dental. If you or your spouse was 65 or older, enter the smaller of Schedule A (Form 1040), line 4, or 2.5% (0.025) of Form 1040, line 38. If zero or less, enter -0-	2	
3	Taxes from Schedule A (Form 1040), line 9	3	
4	Enter the home mortgage interest adjustment, if any, from line 6 of the worksheet in the instructions for this line	4	
5	Miscellaneous deductions from Schedule A (Form 1040), line 27	5	
6	If Form 1040, line 38, is $155,650 or less, enter -0-. Otherwise, see instructions	6	( )
7	Tax refund from Form 1040, line 10 or line 21	7	( )
8	Investment interest expense (difference between regular tax and AMT)	8	
9	Depletion (difference between regular tax and AMT)	9	
10	Net operating loss deduction from Form 1040, line 21. Enter as a positive amount	10	
11	Alternative tax net operating loss deduction	11	( )
12	Interest from specified private activity bonds exempt from the regular tax	12	
13	Qualified small business stock, see instructions	13	
14	Exercise of incentive stock options (excess of AMT income over regular tax income)	14	
15	Estates and trusts (amount from Schedule K-1 (Form 1041), box 12, code A)	15	
16	Electing large partnerships (amount from Schedule K-1 (Form 1065-B), box 6)	16	
17	Disposition of property (difference between AMT and regular tax gain or loss)	17	
18	Depreciation on assets placed in service after 1986 (difference between regular tax and AMT)	18	
19	Passive activities (difference between AMT and regular tax income or loss)	19	
20	Loss limitations (difference between AMT and regular tax income or loss)	20	0
21	Circulation costs (difference between regular tax and AMT)	21	
22	Long-term contracts (difference between AMT and regular tax income)	22	
23	Mining costs (difference between regular tax and AMT)	23	
24	Research and experimental costs (difference between regular tax and AMT)	24	
25	Income from certain installment sales before January 1, 1987	25	( )
26	Intangible drilling costs preference	26	
27	Other adjustments, including income-based related adjustments	27	
28	**Alternative minimum taxable income.** Combine lines 1 through 27. (If married filing separately and line 28 is more than $247,450, see instructions.)	28	127,930

Part II Alternative Minimum Tax (AMT)

29 Exemption. (If you were under age 24 at the end of 2016, see instructions.)

IF your filing status is . . .	**AND line 28 is not over . . .**	**THEN enter on line 29 . . .**
Single or head of household	$119,700	$53,900
Married filing jointly or qualifying widow(er)	159,700	83,800
Married filing separately	79,850	41,900

If line 28 is **over** the amount shown above for your filing status, see instructions. ▶ **29** 51,842

Line	Description	No.	Amount
30	Subtract line 29 from line 28. If more than zero, go to line 31. If zero or less, enter -0- here and on lines 31, 33, and 35, and go to line 34	30	76,088
31	• If you are filing Form 2555 or 2555-EZ, see instructions for the amount to enter. • If you reported capital gain distributions directly on Form 1040, line 13; you reported qualified dividends on Form 1040, line 9b, **or** you had a gain on both lines 15 and 16 of Schedule D (Form 1040) (as refigured for the AMT, if necessary), complete Part III on the back and enter the amount from line 64 here. • **All others:** If line 30 is $186,300 or less ($93,150 or less if married filing separately), multiply line 30 by 26% (0.26). Otherwise, multiply line 30 by 28% (0.28) and subtract $3,726 ($1,863 if married filing separately) from the result.	31	19,783
32	Alternative minimum tax foreign tax credit (see instructions)	32	
33	Tentative minimum tax. Subtract line 32 from line 31	33	19,783
34	Add Form 1040, line 44 (minus any tax from Form 4972), and Form 1040, line 46. Subtract from the result any foreign tax credit from Form 1040, line 48. If you used Schedule J to figure your tax on Form 1040, line 44, refigure that tax without using Schedule J before completing this line (see instructions)	34	24,825
35	**AMT.** Subtract line 34 from line 33. If zero or less, enter -0-. Enter here and on Form 1040, line 45	35	0

For Paperwork Reduction Act Notice, see your tax return instructions.

DAA

EXHIBIT #10

Form 1120S (2017)

Form **1120S**

Department of the Treasury
Internal Revenue Service

U.S. Income Tax Return for an S Corporation

▶ Do not file this form unless the corporation has filed or is attaching Form 2553 to elect to be an S corporation.
▶ Go to *www.irs.gov/Form1120S* for instructions and the latest information.

OMB No. 1545-0123

2017

For calendar year 2017 or tax year beginning , ending

A S election effective date: 01/01/17

B Business activity code number (see instructions):

C Check if Sch. M-3 attached ☐

TYPE OR PRINT

Name:

Number, street, and room or suite no. If a P.O. box, see instructions.

City or town, state or province, country, and ZIP or foreign postal code

D Employer identification number:

E Date incorporated: 02/03/2016

F Total assets (see instructions): $ 9,162

G Is the corporation electing to be an S corporation beginning with this tax year? [X] Yes ☐ No If "Yes," attach Form 2553 if not already filed

H Check if: (1) ☐ Final return (2) ☐ Name change (3) ☐ Address change (4) ☐ Amended return (5) ☐ S election termination or revocation

I Enter the number of shareholders who were shareholders during any part of the tax year ▶ 1

Caution. Include only trade or business income and expenses on lines 1a through 21. See the instructions for more information.

Income	1a	Gross receipts or sales	1a	327,378		
	b	Returns and allowances	1b			
	c	Balance. Subtract line 1b from line 1a			1c	327,378
	2	Cost of goods sold (attach Form 1125-A)			2	
	3	Gross profit. Subtract line 2 from line 1c			3	327,378
	4	Net gain (loss) from Form 4797, line 17 (attach Form 4797)			4	
	5	Other income (loss) (see instructions—attach statement)			5	
	6	**Total income (loss).** Add lines 3 through 5 ▶			6	327,378
Deductions (see instructions for limitations)	7	Compensation of officers (see instructions–attach Form 1125-E)			7	
	8	Salaries and wages (less employment credits)			8	
	9	Repairs and maintenance			9	
	10	Bad debts			10	
	11	Rents			11	
	12	Taxes and licenses			12	908
	13	Interest			13	
	14	Depreciation not claimed on Form 1125-A or elsewhere on return (attach Form 4562)			14	
	15	Depletion **(Do not deduct oil and gas depletion.)**			15	
	16	Advertising			16	
	17	Pension, profit-sharing, etc., plans			17	
	18	Employee benefit programs			18	
	19	Other deductions (attach statement) SEE STMT 1			19	33,633
	20	**Total deductions.** Add lines 7 through 19 ▶			20	34,541
	21	**Ordinary business income (loss).** Subtract line 20 from line 6			21	292,837
Tax and Payments	22a	Excess net passive income or LIFO recapture tax (see instructions)	22a			
	b	Tax from Schedule D (Form 1120S)	22b			
	c	Add lines 22a and 22b (see instructions for additional taxes)			22c	
	23a	2017 estimated tax payments and 2016 overpayment credited to 2017	23a			
	b	Tax deposited with Form 7004	23b			
	c	Credit for federal tax paid on fuels (attach Form 4136)	23c			
	d	Add lines 23a through 23c			23d	
	24	Estimated tax penalty (see instructions). Check if Form 2220 is attached ▶ ☐			24	
	25	**Amount owed.** If line 23d is smaller than the total of lines 22c and 24, enter amount owed			25	
	26	**Overpayment.** If line 23d is larger than the total of lines 22c and 24, enter amount overpaid			26	
	27	Enter amount from line 26 **Credited to 2018 estimated tax** ▶ Refunded ▶			27	

Sign Here

Under penalties of perjury, I declare that I have examined this return, including accompanying schedules and statements, and to the best of my knowledge and belief, it is true, correct, and complete. Declaration of preparer (other than taxpayer) is based on all information of which preparer has any knowledge.

May the IRS discuss this return with the preparer shown below (see instructions)? [X] Yes ☐ No

Signature of officer | Date | Title: PRESIDENT

Paid Preparer Use Only

Print/Type preparer's name | Preparer's signature | Date: 04/14/18 | Check ☐ if self-employed | PTIN

Firm's name ▶ | Firm's EIN ▶

Firm's address ▶ | Phone no.

For Paperwork Reduction Act Notice, see separate instructions.

Form **1120S** (2017)

DAA

Schedule B Other Information (see instructions)

		Yes	No
1	Check accounting method: a [X] Cash b [ ] Accrual c [ ] Other (specify) ▶		
2	See the instructions and enter the: a Business activity ▶ CONSULTING b Product or service ▶ CONSULTING		
3	At any time during the tax year, was any shareholder of the corporation a disregarded entity, a trust, an estate, or a nominee or similar person? If "Yes," attach Schedule B-1, Information on Certain Shareholders of an S Corporation		X
4	At the end of the tax year, did the corporation:		
a	Own directly 20% or more, or own, directly or indirectly, 50% or more of the total stock issued and outstanding of any foreign or domestic corporation? For rules of constructive ownership, see instructions. If "Yes," complete (i) through (v) below		X

(i) Name of Corporation	(ii) Employer Identification Number (if any)	(iii) Country of Incorporation	(iv) Percentage of Stock Owned	(v) If Percentage in (iv) is 100%, Enter the Date (if any) a Qualified Subchapter S Subsidiary Election Was Made

		Yes	No
b	Own directly an interest of 20% or more, or own, directly or indirectly, an interest of 50% or more in the profit, loss, or capital in any foreign or domestic partnership (including an entity treated as a partnership) or in the beneficial interest of a trust? For rules of constructive ownership, see instructions. If "Yes," complete (i) through (v) below		X

(i) Name of Entity	(ii) Employer Identification Number (if any)	(iii) Type of Entity	(iv) Country of Organization	(v) Maximum Percentage Owned in Profit, Loss, or Capital

		Yes	No
5a	At the end of the tax year, did the corporation have any outstanding shares of restricted stock? If "Yes," complete lines (i) and (ii) below.		X
	(i) Total shares of restricted stock ▶		
	(ii) Total shares of non-restricted stock ▶		
b	At the end of the tax year, did the corporation have any outstanding stock options, warrants, or similar instruments? If "Yes," complete lines (i) and (ii) below.		X
	(i) Total shares of stock outstanding at the end of the tax year ▶		
	(ii) Total shares of stock outstanding if all instruments were executed ▶		
6	Has this corporation filed, or is it required to file, Form 8918, Material Advisor Disclosure Statement, to provide information on any reportable transaction?		X
7	Check this box if the corporation issued publicly offered debt instruments with original issue discount ▶ [ ] If checked, the corporation may have to file **Form 8281**, Information Return for Publicly Offered Original Issue Discount Instruments.		
8	If the corporation: (a) was a C corporation before it elected to be an S corporation or the corporation acquired an asset with a basis determined by reference to the basis of the asset (or the basis of any other property) in the hands of a C corporation and (b) has net unrealized built-in gain in excess of the net recognized built-in gain from prior years, enter the net unrealized built-in gain reduced by net recognized built-in gain from prior years (see instructions) ▶ $		
9	Enter the accumulated earnings and profits of the corporation at the end of the tax year. $		
10	Does the corporation satisfy both of the following conditions?		
a	The corporation's total receipts (see instructions) for the tax year were less than $250,000		
b	The corporation's total assets at the end of the tax year were less than $250,000. If "Yes," the corporation is not required to complete Schedules L and M-1.		X
11	During the tax year, did the corporation have any non-shareholder debt that was canceled, was forgiven, or had the terms modified so as to reduce the principal amount of the debt?		X
	If "Yes," enter the amount of principal reduction $		
12	During the tax year, was a qualified subchapter S subsidiary election terminated or revoked? If "Yes," see instructions		X
13a	Did the corporation make any payments in 2017 that would require it to file Form(s) 1099?	X	
b	If "Yes," did the corporation file or will it file required Forms 1099?	X	

Schedule K Shareholders' Pro Rata Share Items

				Total amount
Income (Loss)	1 Ordinary business income (loss) (page 1, line 21)		1	292,837
	2 Net rental real estate income (loss) (attach Form 8825)		2	
	3a Other gross rental income (loss)	3a		
	b Expenses from other rental activities (attach statement)	3b		
	c Other net rental income (loss). Subtract line 3b from line 3a		3c	
	4 Interest income		4	
	5 Dividends: a Ordinary dividends		5a	
	b Qualified dividends	5b		
	6 Royalties		6	
	7 Net short-term capital gain (loss) (attach Schedule D (Form 1120S))		7	
	8a Net long-term capital gain (loss) (attach Schedule D (Form 1120S))		8a	
	b Collectibles (28%) gain (loss)	8b		
	c Unrecaptured section 1250 gain (attach statement)	8c		
	9 Net section 1231 gain (loss) (attach Form 4797)		9	
	10 Other income (loss) (see instructions) Type ▶		10	
Deductions	11 Section 179 deduction (attach Form 4562)		11	8,206
	12a Charitable contributions SEE STMT 2		12a	1,000
	b Investment interest expense		12b	
	c Section 59(e)(2) expenditures (1) Type ▶ (2) Amount ▶		12c(2)	
	d Other deductions (see instructions) Type ▶		12d	
Credits	13a Low-income housing credit (section 42(j)(5))		13a	
	b Low-income housing credit (other)		13b	
	c Qualified rehabilitation expenditures (rental real estate) (attach Form 3468, if applicable)		13c	
	d Other rental real estate credits (see instructions) Type ▶		13d	
	e Other rental credits (see instructions) Type ▶		13e	
	f Biofuel producer credit (attach Form 6478)		13f	
	g Other credits (see instructions) Type ▶		13g	
Foreign Transactions	14a Name of country or U.S. possession ▶			
	b Gross income from all sources		14b	
	c Gross income sourced at shareholder level		14c	
	Foreign gross income sourced at corporate level			
	d Passive category		14d	
	e General category		14e	
	f Other (attach statement)		14f	
	Deductions allocated and apportioned at shareholder level			
	g Interest expense		14g	
	h Other		14h	
	Deductions allocated and apportioned at corporate level to foreign source income			
	i Passive category		14i	
	j General category		14j	
	k Other (attach statement)		14k	
	Other information			
	l Total foreign taxes (check one): ▶ ☐ Paid ☐ Accrued		14l	
	m Reduction in taxes available for credit (attach statement)		14m	
	n Other foreign tax information (attach statement)			
Alternative Minimum Tax (AMT) Items	15a Post-1986 depreciation adjustment		15a	
	b Adjusted gain or loss		15b	
	c Depletion (other than oil and gas)		15c	
	d Oil, gas, and geothermal properties – gross income		15d	
	e Oil, gas, and geothermal properties – deductions		15e	
	f Other AMT items (attach statement)		15f	
Items Affecting Shareholder Basis	16a Tax-exempt interest income		16a	
	b Other tax-exempt income		16b	
	c Nondeductible expenses		16c	
	d Distributions (attach statement if required) (see instructions)		16d	282,589
	e Repayment of loans from shareholders		16e	

DAA

Schedule K — Shareholders' Pro Rata Share Items (continued)

			Total amount
Other Information	17a Investment income	17a	
	b Investment expenses	17b	
	c Dividend distributions paid from accumulated earnings and profits	17c	
	d Other items and amounts (attach statement)		
Recon-ciliation	18 Income/loss reconciliation. Combine the amounts on lines 1 through 10 in the far right column. From the result, subtract the sum of the amounts on lines 11 through 12d and 14l	18	283,631

Schedule L — Balance Sheets per Books

	Beginning of tax year (a)	Beginning of tax year (b)	End of tax year (c)	End of tax year (d)
Assets				
1 Cash				1,542
2a Trade notes and accounts receivable				
b Less allowance for bad debts	( )		( )	
3 Inventories				
4 U.S. government obligations				
5 Tax-exempt securities (see instructions)				
6 Other current assets (attach statement)				
7 Loans to shareholders				
8 Mortgage and real estate loans				
9 Other investments (attach statement)				
10a Buildings and other depreciable assets			8,206	
b Less accumulated depreciation	( )		(586)	7,620
11a Depletable assets				
b Less accumulated depletion	( )		( )	
12 Land (net of any amortization)				
13a Intangible assets (amortizable only)				
b Less accumulated amortization	( )		( )	
14 Other assets (attach statement)				
15 Total assets		0		9,162
Liabilities and Shareholders' Equity				
16 Accounts payable				
17 Mortgages, notes, bonds payable in less than 1 year				
18 Other current liabilities (attach statement)				
19 Loans from shareholders				
20 Mortgages, notes, bonds payable in 1 year or more				
21 Other liabilities (attach statement)				
22 Capital stock				500
23 Additional paid-in capital				
24 Retained earnings				8,662
25 Adjustments to shareholders' equity (attach statement)				
26 Less cost of treasury stock		( )		( )
27 Total liabilities and shareholders' equity		0		9,162

DAA

Schedule M-1 Reconciliation of Income (Loss) per Books With Income (Loss) per Return

Note: The corporation may be required to file Schedule M-3 (see instructions)

1	Net income (loss) per books	291,251	5	Income recorded on books this year not included on Schedule K, lines 1 through 10 (itemize): a Tax-exempt interest $	
2	Income included on Schedule K, lines 1, 2, 3c, 4, 5a, 6, 7, 8a, 9, and 10, not recorded on books this year (itemize)				
3	Expenses recorded on books this year not included on Schedule K, lines 1 through 12 and 14l (itemize): a Depreciation $ b Travel and entertainment $		6	Deductions included on Schedule K, lines 1 through 12 and 14l, not charged against book income this year (itemize): a Depreciation $ 7,620	7,620
			7	Add lines 5 and 6	7,620
4	Add lines 1 through 3	291,251	8	Income (loss) (Schedule K, line 18). Line 4 less line 7	283,631

Schedule M-2 Analysis of Accumulated Adjustments Account, Other Adjustments Account, and Shareholders' Undistributed Taxable Income Previously Taxed (see instructions)

		(a) Accumulated adjustments account	(b) Other adjustments account	(c) Shareholders' undistributed taxable income previously taxed
1	Balance at beginning of tax year			
2	Ordinary income from page 1, line 21	292,837		
3	Other additions			
4	Loss from page 1, line 21	( )		
5	Other reductions STMT 3	(9,206)	( )	
6	Combine lines 1 through 5	283,631		
7	Distributions other than dividend distributions	282,589		
8	Balance at end of tax year. Subtract line 7 from line 6	1,042		

671117

☐ Final K-1 ☐ Amended K-1 OMB No. 1545-0123

Schedule K-1 (Form 1120S) 2017

Department of the Treasury
Internal Revenue Service

For calendar year 2017, or tax year

beginning ______ ending ______

Shareholder's Share of Income, Deductions, Credits, etc.

▶ See back of form and separate instructions.

Part I Information About the Corporation

A Corporation's employer identification number

[redacted]

B Corporation's name, address, city, state, and ZIP code

CONSULTANTS FOR AMERICA'S VETERANS

[redacted]

C IRS Center where corporation filed return

E-FILE

Part II Information About the Shareholder

D Shareholder's identifying number

[redacted]

E Shareholder's name, address, city, state, and ZIP code

[redacted]

[redacted] CA 92123

F Shareholder's percentage of stock ownership for tax year .... 100.000000 %

For IRS Use Only

Part III Shareholder's Share of Current Year Income, Deductions, Credits, and Other Items

1	Ordinary business income (loss)	292,837	13	Credits	
2	Net rental real estate income (loss)				
3	Other net rental income (loss)				
4	Interest income				
5a	Ordinary dividends				
5b	Qualified dividends		14	Foreign transactions	
6	Royalties				
7	Net short-term capital gain (loss)				
8a	Net long-term capital gain (loss)				
8b	Collectibles (28%) gain (loss)				
8c	Unrecaptured section 1250 gain				
9	Net section 1231 gain (loss)				
10	Other income (loss)		15	Alternative minimum tax (AMT) items	
11	Section 179 deduction	8,206	16	Items affecting shareholder basis	D 282,589
12	Other deductions	A 1,000			
			17	Other information	

* See attached statement for additional information.

EXHIBIT #11

Form 4562

Form **4562**

Department of the Treasury
Internal Revenue Service (99)

Depreciation and Amortization

(Including Information on Listed Property)

▶ Attach to your tax return.

▶ Go to *www.irs.gov/Form4562* for instructions and the latest information.

OMB No. 1545-0172

2017

Attachment Sequence No. 179

Name(s) shown on return: [redacted]

Identifying number: [redacted]

Business or activity to which this form relates: REGULAR DEPRECIATION

Part I Election To Expense Certain Property Under Section 179

Note: If you have any listed property, complete Part V before you complete Part I.

1	Maximum amount (see instructions)	1	510,000
2	Total cost of section 179 property placed in service (see instructions)	2	8,206
3	Threshold cost of section 179 property before reduction in limitation (see instructions)	3	2,030,000
4	Reduction in limitation. Subtract line 3 from line 2. If zero or less, enter -0-	4	0
5	Dollar limitation for tax year. Subtract line 4 from line 1. If zero or less, enter -0-. If married filing separately, see instructions	5	510,000

6	(a) Description of property	(b) Cost (business use only)	(c) Elected cost
	FURNITURE & FIXTURES	8,206	8,206

7	Listed property. Enter the amount from line 29	7	
8	Total elected cost of section 179 property. Add amounts in column (c), lines 6 and 7	8	8,206
9	Tentative deduction. Enter the smaller of line 5 or line 8	9	8,206
10	Carryover of disallowed deduction from line 13 of your 2016 Form 4562	10	
11	Business income limitation. Enter the smaller of business income (not less than zero) or line 5 (see instructions)	11	292,837
12	Section 179 expense deduction. Add lines 9 and 10, but don't enter more than line 11	12	8,206
13	Carryover of disallowed deduction to 2018. Add lines 9 and 10, less line 12 ▶	13	

Note: Don't use Part II or Part III below for listed property. Instead, use Part V.

Part II Special Depreciation Allowance and Other Depreciation (Don't include listed property.) (See instructions.)

14	Special depreciation allowance for qualified property (other than listed property) placed in service during the tax year (see instructions)	14	
15	Property subject to section 168(f)(1) election	15	
16	Other depreciation (including ACRS)	16	

Part III MACRS Depreciation (Don't include listed property.) (See instructions.)

Section A

17	MACRS deductions for assets placed in service in tax years beginning before 2017	17	0
18	If you are electing to group any assets placed in service during the tax year into one or more general asset accounts, check here ▶ ☐		

Section B—Assets Placed in Service During 2017 Tax Year Using the General Depreciation System

(a) Classification of property	(b) Month and year placed in service	(c) Basis for depreciation (business/investment use only—see instructions)	(d) Recovery period	(e) Convention	(f) Method	(g) Depreciation deduction
19a 3-year property						
b 5-year property						
c 7-year property						
d 10-year property						
e 15-year property						
f 20-year property						
g 25-year property			25 yrs.		S/L	
h Residential rental property			27.5 yrs.	MM	S/L	
			27.5 yrs.	MM	S/L	
i Nonresidential real property			39 yrs.	MM	S/L	
				MM	S/L	

Section C—Assets Placed in Service During 2017 Tax Year Using the Alternative Depreciation System

(a) Classification of property	(b)	(c)	(d)	(e)	(f)	(g)
20a Class life					S/L	
b 12-year			12 yrs.		S/L	
c 40-year			40 yrs.	MM	S/L	

Part IV Summary (See instructions.)

21	Listed property. Enter amount from line 28	21	
22	Total. Add amounts from line 12, lines 14 through 17, lines 19 and 20 in column (g), and line 21. Enter here and on the appropriate lines of your return. Partnerships and S corporations—see instructions	22	
23	For assets shown above and placed in service during the current year, enter the portion of the basis attributable to section 263A costs	23	

For Paperwork Reduction Act Notice, see separate instructions.

DAA

THERE ARE NO AMOUNTS FOR PAGE 2

EXHIBIT #12

Detailed Job Report for Public Relation Specialists

O*NET OnLine

Updated 2018

green

Details Report for:

27-3031.00 - Public Relations Specialists

Engage in promoting or creating an intended public image for individuals, groups, or organizations. May write or select material for release to various communications media.

Sample of reported job titles: Account Executive, Communications Director, Communications Specialist, Corporate Communications Specialist, Media Relations Specialist, Public Affairs Specialist, Public Information Officer, Public Information Specialist, Public Relations Coordinator, Public Relations Specialist (PR Specialist)

View report: Summary | Details | Custom

Tasks | Technology Skills | Tools Used | Knowledge | Skills | Abilities | Work Activities | Detailed Work Activities | Work Context | Job Zone | Education | Credentials | Interests | Work Styles | Work Values | Related Occupations | Wages & Employment | Job Openings | Additional Information

Tasks

Save Table (XLS/CSV)

10 of 18 displayed (16 important)

Importance	Category	Task
86	Core	Respond to requests for information from the media or designate an appropriate spokesperson or information source.
83	Core	Write press releases or other media communications to promote clients.
79	Core	Establish or maintain cooperative relationships with representatives of community, consumer, employee, or public interest groups.
77	Core	Plan or direct development or communication of programs to maintain favorable public or stockholder perceptions of an organization's accomplishments, agenda, or environmental responsibility.
75	Core	Study the objectives, promotional policies, or needs of organizations to develop public relations strategies that will influence public opinion or promote ideas, products, or services.
72	Core	Coach client representatives in effective communication with the public or with employees.
71	Core	Update and maintain content posted on the Web.
71	Core	Confer with other managers to identify trends or key group interests or concerns or to provide advice on business decisions.
69	Core	Prepare or edit organizational publications, such as employee newsletters or stockholders' reports, for internal or external audiences.
64	Core	Coordinate public responses to environmental management incidents or conflicts.

back to top

Technology Skills

Save Table (XLS/CSV)

10 of 21 displayed

- **Customer relationship management CRM software** — Blackbaud The Raiser's Edge ; Oracle Eloqua ;

Salesforce software 🔥

- **Data base user interface and query software** — Cision CisionPoint; FileMaker Pro 🔥; Google+; LinkedIn 🔥
- **Desktop publishing software** — Adobe Systems Adobe InDesign 🔥; Microsoft Publisher 🔥
- **Document management software** — Adobe Systems Adobe Acrobat 🔥; Adobe Systems Adobe Reader
- **Graphics or photo imaging software** — Adobe Systems Adobe Creative Cloud 🔥; Adobe Systems Adobe Illustrator 🔥; Adobe Systems Adobe Photoshop 🔥; Apple iPhoto (see all 6 examples)
- **Sales and marketing software** — Google AdWords 🔥; Marketo Marketing Automation 🔥
- **Video creation and editing software** — Adobe Systems Adobe AfterEffects 🔥; Apple Final Cut Pro 🔥; Apple QuickTime; YouTube 🔥 (see all 5 examples)
- **Web page creation and editing software** — Adobe Systems Adobe Dreamweaver 🔥; Facebook 🔥; Podcasting software; Website management software (see all 6 examples)
- **Web platform development software** — Cascading Style Sheets CSS 🔥; Drupal 🔥; Dynamic hypertext markup language DHTML 🔥; JavaScript 🔥 (see all 6 examples)
- **Word processing software** — Adobe Systems Adobe Writer; Microsoft Word 🔥

🔥 Hot Technology — a technology requirement frequently included in employer job postings.

back to top

Tools Used Save Table (XLS/CSV)

All 6 displayed

- **Desktop computers**
- **Laser printers** — Computer laser printers
- **Notebook computers** — Laptop computers
- **Personal computers**
- **Photocopiers** — Photocopying equipment
- **Special purpose telephones** — Multi-line telephone systems

back to top

Knowledge Save Table (XLS/CSV)

10 of 33 displayed (7 important)

Importance	Knowledge
99	**Communications and Media** — Knowledge of media production, communication, and dissemination techniques and methods. This includes alternative ways to inform and entertain via written, oral, and visual media.
99	**English Language** — Knowledge of the structure and content of the English language including the meaning and spelling of words, rules of composition, and grammar.
63	**Sales and Marketing** — Knowledge of principles and methods for showing, promoting, and selling products or services. This includes marketing strategy and tactics, product demonstration, sales techniques, and sales control systems.
62	**Customer and Personal Service** — Knowledge of principles and processes for providing customer and personal services. This includes customer needs assessment, meeting quality standards for services, and evaluation of customer satisfaction.
60	**Administration and Management** — Knowledge of business and management principles involved in strategic planning, resource allocation, human resources modeling, leadership

technique, production methods, and coordination of people and resources.

Importance	Knowledge
57	**Computers and Electronics** — Knowledge of circuit boards, processors, chips, electronic equipment, and computer hardware and software, including applications and programming.
52	**Clerical** — Knowledge of administrative and clerical procedures and systems such as word processing, managing files and records, stenography and transcription, designing forms, and other office procedures and terminology.
45	**Sociology and Anthropology** — Knowledge of group behavior and dynamics, societal trends and influences, human migrations, ethnicity, cultures and their history and origins.
44	**Law and Government** — Knowledge of laws, legal codes, court procedures, precedents, government regulations, executive orders, agency rules, and the democratic political process.
43	**Education and Training** — Knowledge of principles and methods for curriculum and training design, teaching and instruction for individuals and groups, and the measurement of training effects.

back to top

Skills Save Table (XLS/CSV)

10 of 35 displayed (18 important)

Importance	Skill
78	**Active Listening** — Giving full attention to what other people are saying, taking time to understand the points being made, asking questions as appropriate, and not interrupting at inappropriate times.
78	**Speaking** — Talking to others to convey information effectively.
75	**Coordination** — Adjusting actions in relation to others' actions.
75	**Social Perceptiveness** — Being aware of others' reactions and understanding why they react as they do.
75	**Time Management** — Managing one's own time and the time of others.
75	**Writing** — Communicating effectively in writing as appropriate for the needs of the audience.
72	**Critical Thinking** — Using logic and reasoning to identify the strengths and weaknesses of alternative solutions, conclusions or approaches to problems.
72	**Reading Comprehension** — Understanding written sentences and paragraphs in work related documents.
66	**Persuasion** — Persuading others to change their minds or behavior.
63	**Complex Problem Solving** — Identifying complex problems and reviewing related information to develop and evaluate options and implement solutions.

back to top

Abilities Save Table (XLS/CSV)

10 of 52 displayed (15 important)

Importance	Ability
85	**Oral Comprehension** — The ability to listen to and understand information and ideas presented through spoken words and sentences.
81	**Oral Expression** — The ability to communicate information and ideas in speaking so others will understand.
75	**Speech Clarity** — The ability to speak clearly so others can understand you.

75 ⊕ **Written Expression** — The ability to communicate information and ideas in writing so others will understand.

72 ⊕ **Speech Recognition** — The ability to identify and understand the speech of another person.

72 ⊕ **Written Comprehension** — The ability to read and understand information and ideas presented in writing.

69 ⊕ **Deductive Reasoning** — The ability to apply general rules to specific problems to produce answers that make sense.

69 ⊕ **Near Vision** — The ability to see details at close range (within a few feet of the observer).

69 ⊕ **Problem Sensitivity** — The ability to tell when something is wrong or is likely to go wrong. It does not involve solving the problem, only recognizing there is a problem.

66 ⊕ **Inductive Reasoning** — The ability to combine pieces of information to form general rules or conclusions (includes finding a relationship among seemingly unrelated events).

back to top

Work Activities Save Table (XLS/CSV)

10 of 41 displayed (29 important)

Importance	Work Activity
96	**Getting Information** — Observing, receiving, and otherwise obtaining information from all relevant sources.
95	**Communicating with Persons Outside Organization** — Communicating with people outside the organization, representing the organization to customers, the public, government, and other external sources. This information can be exchanged in person, in writing, or by telephone or e-mail.
90	**Communicating with Supervisors, Peers, or Subordinates** — Providing information to supervisors, co-workers, and subordinates by telephone, in written form, e-mail, or in person.
89	**Interacting With Computers** — Using computers and computer systems (including hardware and software) to program, write software, set up functions, enter data, or process information.
87	**Thinking Creatively** — Developing, designing, or creating new applications, ideas, relationships, systems, or products, including artistic contributions.
86	**Establishing and Maintaining Interpersonal Relationships** — Developing constructive and cooperative working relationships with others, and maintaining them over time.
83	**Developing Objectives and Strategies** — Establishing long-range objectives and specifying the strategies and actions to achieve them.
82	**Updating and Using Relevant Knowledge** — Keeping up-to-date technically and applying new knowledge to your job.
81	**Making Decisions and Solving Problems** — Analyzing information and evaluating results to choose the best solution and solve problems.
81	**Organizing, Planning, and Prioritizing Work** — Developing specific goals and plans to prioritize, organize, and accomplish your work.

back to top

Detailed Work Activities Save Table (XLS/CSV)

10 of 11 displayed

- Provide educational information to the public.
- Write advertising or promotional material.

- Develop promotional strategies or plans.
- Coach others.
- Collaborate with others in marketing activities.
- Write informational material.
- Edit written materials.
- Coordinate logistics for productions or events.
- Conduct market research.
- Inform viewers, listeners, or audiences.

back to top

Work Context Save Table (XLS/CSV)

10 of 57 displayed

Work Context	Percentage of Top Responses
Electronic Mail — How often do you use electronic mail in this job?	100 Every day
Telephone — How often do you have telephone conversations in this job?	100 Every day
Face-to-Face Discussions — How often do you have to have face-to-face discussions with individuals or teams in this job?	75 Every day 25 Once a week or more but not every day
Indoors, Environmentally Controlled — How often does this job require working indoors in environmentally controlled conditions?	88 Every day
Contact With Others — How much does this job require the worker to be in contact with others (face-to-face, by telephone, or otherwise) in order to perform it?	67 Constant contact with others 29 Contact with others most of the time
Spend Time Sitting — How much does this job require sitting?	54 Continually or almost continually 42 More than half the time
Time Pressure — How often does this job require the worker to meet strict deadlines?	46 Every day 46 Once a week or more but not every day
Work With Work Group or Team — How important is it to work with others in a group or team in this job?	58 Extremely important 21 Very important 21 Important
Duration of Typical Work Week — Number of hours typically worked in one week.	61 More than 40 hours 39 40 hours
Importance of Being Exact or Accurate — How important is being very exact or highly accurate in performing this job?	42 Extremely important 38 Very important 21 Important

back to top

Job Zone Save Table (XLS/CSV)

Title	Job Zone Four: Considerable Preparation Needed
Education	Most of these occupations require a four-year bachelor's degree, but some do not.
Related Experience	A considerable amount of work-related skill, knowledge, or experience is needed for these occupations. For example, an accountant must complete four years of college and work for several years in accounting to be considered qualified.
Job Training	Employees in these occupations usually need several years of work-related experience, on-the-job training, and/or vocational training.
Job Zone Examples	Many of these occupations involve coordinating, supervising, managing, or training others. Examples include accountants, sales managers, database administrators, graphic designers, chemists, art directors, and cost estimators.
SVP Range	(7.0 to < 8.0)

back to top

Education

Percentage of Respondents	Education Level Required
92	Bachelor's degree
8	Master's degree

back to top

Credentials

Find Training | Find Certifications | Find Licenses | Find Apprenticeships

back to top

Interests

Save Table (XLS/CSV)

All 6 displayed (3 important)

Occupational Interest	Interest
100	**Enterprising** — Enterprising occupations frequently involve starting up and carrying out projects. These occupations can involve leading people and making many decisions. Sometimes they require risk taking and often deal with business.
67	**Artistic** — Artistic occupations frequently involve working with forms, designs and patterns. They often require self-expression and the work can be done without following a clear set of rules.
61	**Social** — Social occupations frequently involve working with, communicating with, and teaching people. These occupations often involve helping or providing service to others.
33	**Conventional** — Conventional occupations frequently involve following set procedures and routines. These occupations can include working with data and details more than with ideas. Usually there is a clear line of authority to follow.
17	**Investigative** — Investigative occupations frequently involve working with ideas, and require an extensive amount of thinking. These occupations can involve searching for facts and figuring out problems mentally.
0	**Realistic** — Realistic occupations frequently involve work activities that include practical, hands-on problems and solutions. They often deal with plants, animals, and real-world materials like

wood, tools, and machinery. Many of the occupations require working outside, and do not involve a lot of paperwork or working closely with others.

back to top

Work Styles Save Table (XLS/CSV)

10 of 16 displayed (16 important)

Importance	Work Style
92	**Integrity** — Job requires being honest and ethical.
91	**Attention to Detail** — Job requires being careful about detail and thorough in completing work tasks.
88	**Dependability** — Job requires being reliable, responsible, and dependable, and fulfilling obligations.
88	**Persistence** — Job requires persistence in the face of obstacles.
86	**Cooperation** — Job requires being pleasant with others on the job and displaying a good-natured, cooperative attitude.
86	**Stress Tolerance** — Job requires accepting criticism and dealing calmly and effectively with high stress situations.
85	**Initiative** — Job requires a willingness to take on responsibilities and challenges.
82	**Adaptability/Flexibility** — Job requires being open to change (positive or negative) and to considerable variety in the workplace.
81	**Self Control** — Job requires maintaining composure, keeping emotions in check, controlling anger, and avoiding aggressive behavior, even in very difficult situations.
77	**Achievement/Effort** — Job requires establishing and maintaining personally challenging achievement goals and exerting effort toward mastering tasks.

back to top

Work Values Save Table (XLS/CSV)

All 6 displayed (6 important)

Extent	Work Value
78	**Achievement** — Occupations that satisfy this work value are results oriented and allow employees to use their strongest abilities, giving them a feeling of accomplishment. Corresponding needs are Ability Utilization and Achievement.
78	**Independence** — Occupations that satisfy this work value allow employees to work on their own and make decisions. Corresponding needs are Creativity, Responsibility and Autonomy.
72	**Relationships** — Occupations that satisfy this work value allow employees to provide service to others and work with co-workers in a friendly non-competitive environment. Corresponding needs are Co-workers, Moral Values and Social Service.
72	**Working Conditions** — Occupations that satisfy this work value offer job security and good working conditions. Corresponding needs are Activity, Compensation, Independence, Security, Variety and Working Conditions.
61	**Recognition** — Occupations that satisfy this work value offer advancement, potential for leadership, and are often considered prestigious. Corresponding needs are Advancement, Authority, Recognition and Social Status.
61	**Support** — Occupations that satisfy this work value offer supportive management that stands behind employees. Corresponding needs are Company Policies, Supervision: Human Relations

and Supervision: Technical.

back to top

Related Occupations Save Table (XLS/CSV)

All 9 displayed

11-2011.00	Advertising and Promotions Managers
11-2031.00	Public Relations and Fundraising Managers
13-1121.00	Meeting, Convention, and Event Planners
13-1161.00	Market Research Analysts and Marketing Specialists Bright Outlook
23-1022.00	Arbitrators, Mediators, and Conciliators Green
27-3043.04	Copy Writers
41-3011.00	Advertising Sales Agents
41-3021.00	Insurance Sales Agents
41-3031.02	Sales Agents, Financial Services

back to top

Wages & Employment Trends

Median wages (2017)	$28.51 hourly, $59,300 annual
State wages	Local Salary Info
Employment (2016)	260,000 employees
Projected growth (2016-2026)	Average (5% to 9%)
Projected job openings (2016-2026)	28,200
State trends	Employment Trends
Top industries (2016)	Other Services (Except Public Administration) (23% employed in this sector) Professional, Scientific, and Technical Services (22%) Educational Services (11%) (see all industries)

Source: Bureau of Labor Statistics 2017 wage data and 2016-2026 employment projections. "Projected growth" represents the estimated change in total employment over the projections period (2016-2026). "Projected job openings" represent openings due to growth and replacement.

back to top

Job Openings on the Web

Find Jobs

back to top

Sources of Additional Information

All 1 displayed

Disclaimer: Sources are listed to provide additional information on related jobs, specialties, and/or industries. Links to non-DOL Internet sites are provided for your convenience and do not constitute an endorsement.

- Occupational Outlook Handbook: Public relations specialists

back to top

EXHIBIT #13

Job Zones Overview

O*NET OnLine

O*NET OnLine Help

Job Zones

Overview

A Job Zone is a group of occupations that are similar in:

- how much education people need to do the work,
- how much related experience people need to do the work, and
- how much on-the-job training people need to do the work.

The five Job Zones are:

- Job Zone 1 - occupations that need little or no preparation
- Job Zone 2 - occupations that need some preparation
- Job Zone 3 - occupations that need medium preparation
- Job Zone 4 - occupations that need considerable preparation
- Job Zone 5 - occupations that need extensive preparation

Job Zone One: Little or No Preparation Needed

Education	Some of these occupations may require a high school diploma or GED certificate.
Related Experience	Little or no previous work-related skill, knowledge, or experience is needed for these occupations. For example, a person can become a waiter or waitress even if he/she has never worked before.
Job Training	Employees in these occupations need anywhere from a few days to a few months of training. Usually, an experienced worker could show you how to do the job.
Job Zone Examples	These occupations involve following instructions and helping others. Examples include counter and rental clerks, dishwashers, cashiers, landscaping and groundskeeping workers, logging equipment operators, and baristas.
SVP Range	(Below 4.0)

Job Zone Two: Some Preparation Needed

Education	These occupations usually require a high school diploma.
Related Experience	Some previous work-related skill, knowledge, or experience is usually needed. For example, a teller would benefit from experience working directly with the public.
Job Training	Employees in these occupations need anywhere from a few months to one year of working with experienced employees. A recognized apprenticeship program may be associated with these occupations.
Job Zone Examples	These occupations often involve using your knowledge and skills to help others. Examples include orderlies, forest firefighters, customer service representatives, security guards, upholsterers, and tellers.
SVP Range	(4.0 to < 6.0)

Job Zone Three: Medium Preparation Needed

Education Most occupations in this zone require training in vocational schools, related on-the-job experience, or an associate's degree.

Related Experience Previous work-related skill, knowledge, or experience is required for these occupations. For example, an electrician must have completed three or four years of apprenticeship or several years of vocational training, and often must have passed a licensing exam, in order to perform the job.

Job Training Employees in these occupations usually need one or two years of training involving both on-the-job experience and informal training with experienced workers. A recognized apprenticeship program may be associated with these occupations.

Job Zone Examples These occupations usually involve using communication and organizational skills to coordinate, supervise, manage, or train others to accomplish goals. Examples include hydroelectric production managers, travel guides, electricians, agricultural technicians, barbers, nannies, and medical assistants.

SVP Range (6.0 to < 7.0)

Job Zone Four: Considerable Preparation Needed

Education Most of these occupations require a four-year bachelor's degree, but some do not.

Related Experience A considerable amount of work-related skill, knowledge, or experience is needed for these occupations. For example, an accountant must complete four years of college and work for several years in accounting to be considered qualified.

Job Training Employees in these occupations usually need several years of work-related experience, on-the-job training, and/or vocational training.

Job Zone Examples Many of these occupations involve coordinating, supervising, managing, or training others. Examples include accountants, sales managers, database administrators, graphic designers, chemists, art directors, and cost estimators.

SVP Range (7.0 to < 8.0)

Job Zone Five: Extensive Preparation Needed

Education Most of these occupations require graduate school. For example, they may require a master's degree, and some require a Ph.D., M.D., or J.D. (law degree).

Related Experience Extensive skill, knowledge, and experience are needed for these occupations. Many require more than five years of experience. For example, surgeons must complete four years of college and an additional five to seven years of specialized medical training to be able to do their job.

Job Training Employees may need some on-the-job training, but most of these occupations assume that the person will already have the required skills, knowledge, work-related experience, and/or training.

Job Zone Examples These occupations often involve coordinating, training, supervising, or managing the activities of others to accomplish goals. Very advanced communication and organizational skills are required. Examples include librarians, lawyers, astronomers, biologists, clergy, surgeons, and veterinarians.

SVP Range (8.0 and above)

Previous: Scales, Ratings, and Standardized Scores
Next: Specific Vocational Preparation (SVP)

back to OnLine Help table of contents

EXHIBIT #14

Specific Vocational Preparation

O*NET OnLine

O*NET OnLine Help

Specific Vocational Preparation (SVP)

Specific Vocational Preparation is a component of Worker Characteristics information found in the *Dictionary of Occupational Titles* (U.S. Department of Labor, 1991).

Specific Vocational Preparation, as defined in Appendix C of the *Dictionary of Occupational Titles*, is the amount of lapsed time required by a typical worker to learn the techniques, acquire the information, and develop the facility needed for average performance in a specific job-worker situation.

This training may be acquired in a school, work, military, institutional, or vocational environment. It does not include the orientation time required of a fully qualified worker to become accustomed to the special conditions of any new job. Specific vocational training includes: vocational education, apprenticeship training, in-plant training, on-the-job training, and essential experience in other jobs.

Specific vocational training includes training given in any of the following circumstances:

1. Vocational education (high school, commercial or shop training, technical school, art school, and that part of college training which is organized around a specific vocational objective)
2. Apprenticeship training (for apprenticeable jobs only)
3. In-plant training (organized classroom study provided by an employer)
4. On-the-job training (serving as learner or trainee on the job under the instruction of a qualified worker)
5. Essential experience in other jobs (serving in less responsible jobs, which lead to the higher-grade job, or serving in other jobs which qualify).

The following is an explanation of the various levels of specific vocational preparation:

Level Time

1. Short demonstration only
2. Anything beyond short demonstration up to and including 1 month
3. Over 1 month up to and including 3 months
4. Over 3 months up to and including 6 months
5. Over 6 months up to and including 1 year
6. Over 1 year up to and including 2 years
7. Over 2 years up to and including 4 years
8. Over 4 years up to and including 10 years
9. Over 10 years

Note: The levels of this scale are mutually exclusive and do not overlap.

U.S. Department of Labor. (1991). *Dictionary of Occupational Titles* (Rev. 4th ed.). Washington, DC: U.S. Government Printing Office.

Previous: Job Zones
Next: Data Collection Information

back to OnLine Help table of contents

EXHIBIT #15

Applicant's Birth Certificate

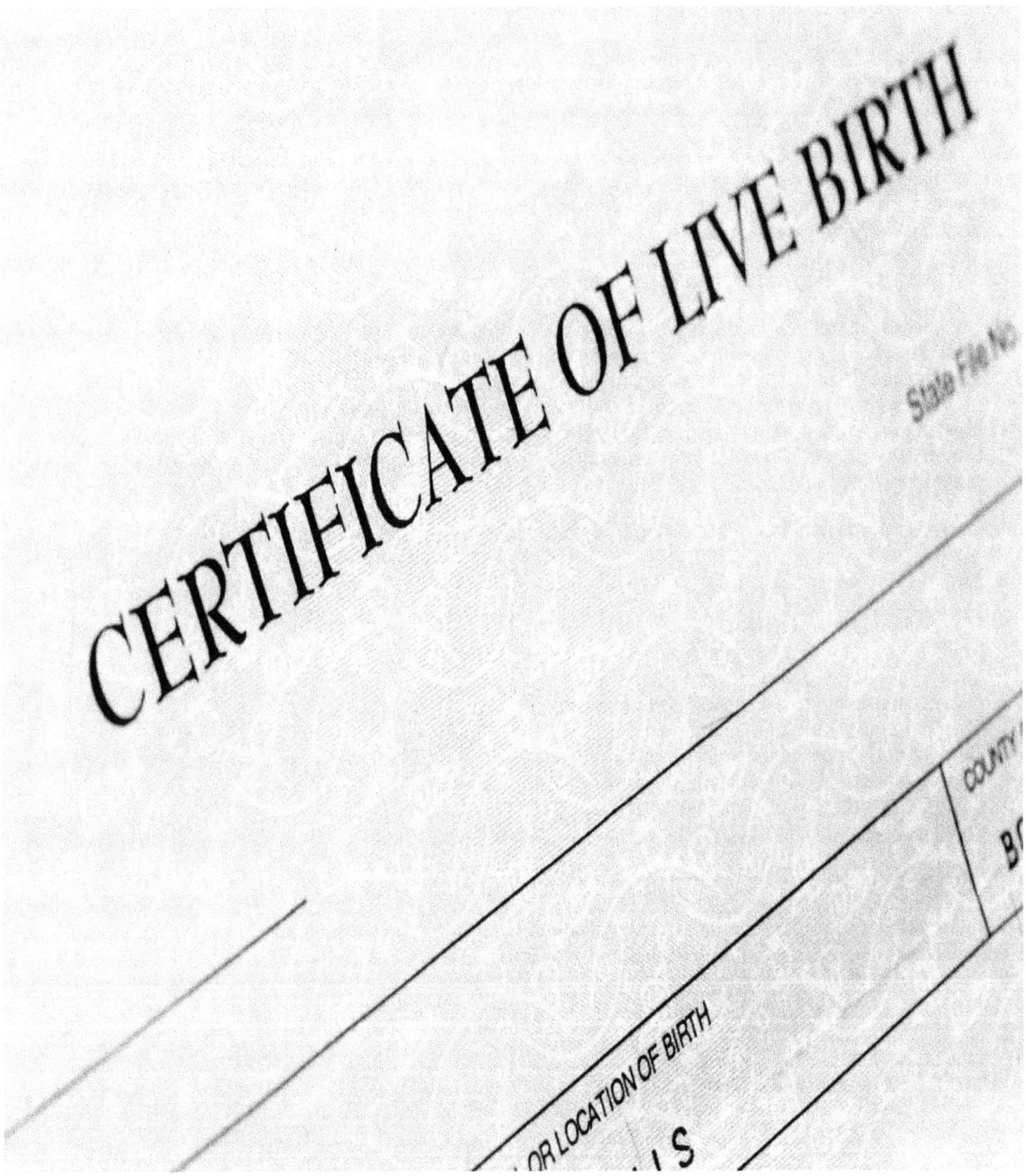

משרד הפנים
وزارة الداخلية
MINISTRY OF THE INTERIOR

מדינת ישראל
دولة اسرائيل
STATE OF ISRAEL

תעודת לידה
BIRTH CERTIFICATE

Surname	ישראלי	שם המשפחה
Given name	מרסל	השם הפרטי
Given name of father	יעקב	השם הפרטי של האב
Given name of mother	זהבה	השם הפרטי של האם
Surname of mother's father	עוזר	שם המשפחה של אבי האם
Identity no.	0 2178242 0	מספר זהות
Sex	נקבה	המין
Nationality	יהודי	הלאום
Religion	יהודי	הדת
Place of birth	תל אביב - יפו	מקום הלידה
Hospital's name	בית היולדות	שם בית החולים
Date of birth	7 במאי 1983	תאריך הלידה

I hereby certify that the above newborn is listed in the Births Register.

This certificate is issued in accordance with article 30 of the Population Registry Law of 1965

Ministry of Foreign Affairs in Jerusalem

Authority

Date 13 October 2013

הנני מאשר כי הילוד נרשם בספר הלידות

התעודה ניתנה בהתאם לסעיף 30

לחוק מרשם האוכלוסין תשכ"ה - 1965

במשרד החוץ בירושלים

בתאריך 13 באוקטובר 2013

חותמת המשרד
Seal of Ministry

בן שמעון אורית
משרד החוץ

שם וחתימת הפקיד
Name and Signature of registrar

לכבוד

מרסל ישראלי

הרצל 135

תל אביב - יפו 6810104

APOSTILLE
(Convention de La Haye du 5 octobre 1961)

1. STATE OF ISRAEL		.1 מדינת ישראל
2. THIS PUBLIC DOCUMENT HAS BEEN SIGNED BY MR /MS	בן-שמעון אורית BEN-SHIMON ORIT	.2 מסמך ציבורי זה נחתם בידי מר/גב'
3. ACTING IN THE CAPACITY OF **HEAD OF DOCUMENTATION BRANCH**		.3 המכהן בתור ר' ענף תיעוד
4. BEARS THE SEAL/STAMP OF THE MINISTRY OF	משרד החוץ FOREIGN AFFAIRS	.4 נושא את החותם/חותמת של משרד
5. CERTIFIED AT THE MINISTRY OF FOREIGN AFFAIRS		.5 אושר במשרד החוץ
6. THE	14/10/2013	.6 ביום
7. BY	GUY HAVRY גיא חעברי	.7 על-ידי
8 NO 702511		8 מס' 702511
9. SEAL/STAMP	משרד החוץ · MINISTRY OF FOREIGN AFFAIRS	.9 חותם/חותמת
10 SIGNATURE JERUSALEM		.10 חתימה, ירושלים

EXHIBIT #16

Applicant's Passport

PASSPORT דרכון STATE OF ISRAEL מדינת ישראל

Type / סוג
P / ד

Code of State / סמל המדינה
ISR

Passport No. / מס׳ דרכון
20889488

Surname

שם משפחה
ישראלי

Given name

שם פרטי
מרסל

Nationality

אזרחות
ישראלית

Date of birth / תאריך לידה
07/05/1983

I.D. No. / מס׳ זהות
0-2178242-0

Sex / מין

Place of birth

מקום לידה
ישראל

Date of issue / תאריך הוצאה

Date of expiry / תאריך פקיעת תוקף
07/08/2023

Authority - I.C. Passport at-

סמכות - ממונה דרכונים ב-
לוס אנגילס

P<ISRISRAELI<< <<<<<<<<<<<<<<<<<<<<<<<<

20889488<9ISR8305077F23080760<2178242<0<<<64

EXHIBIT #17

Applicant's Resume

LOREM IPSUM

DOLOR SIT AMET

ABOUT ME

Lorem ipsum dolor sit amet, consecte adipiscing elit. Phasellus bibendum, turpis et cursus aliquam, nulla lectus bibendum leo, ut dapibus neque orci sit amet justo. Nam bibendum nisl euismod, blandit diam eu, aliquam tortor. Nam interdum nisi ut erat efficitur rhoncus. Nullam ut pulvinar urna, eu fringilla mi. Vivamus nec accumsan libero, ut malesuada dolor.

CONTACT ME

+123 456 789

info@loremipsum.com

loremipsum.com

SKILLS

LOREM

IPSUM

SIT

EDUCATION

LOREM
2012-2013
LOREM IPSUM
Lorem ipsum dolor sit amet, consectetur adipiscing elit. Phasellus bibendum

IPSUM
2010-2012
LOREM IPSUM
Lorem ipsum dolor sit amet, consectetur adipiscing elit. Phasellus bibendum.

SIT AMET
2008-2010
LOREM IPSUM
Lorem ipsum dolor sit amet, consectetur adipiscing elit. Phasellus bibendum

EXPERIENCE

LOREM
2010-2015
LOREM IPSUM DOLOR
Lorem ipsum dolor sit amet, consectetur adipiscing elit. Phasellus bibendum, turpis et cursus aliquam, nulla lectus bibendum leo, ut dapibus neque orci sit am.

IPSUM
2010-2015
LOREM IPSUM DOLOR
Lorem ipsum dolor sit amet, consectetur adipiscing elit. Phasellus bibendum, turpis et cursus aliquam, nulla lectus bibendum leo, ut dapibus neque orci sit am.

DOLOR
2010-2015
LOREM IPSUM DOLOR
Lorem ipsum dolor sit amet, consectetur adipiscing elit. Phasellus bibendum, turpis et cursus aliquam, nulla lectus bibendum leo, ut dapibus neque orci sit am.

SIT AMET
2010-2015
LOREM IPSUM DOLOR
Lorem ipsum dolor sit amet, consectetur adipiscing elit. Phasellus bibendum, turpis et cursus aliquam, nulla lectus bibendum leo, ut dapibus neque orci sit am.

PROFESSIONAL SKILLS

LOREM

IPSUM

DOLOR

SIT AMET

PERSONAL SKILLS

LOREM

IPSUM

DOLOR

SIT AMET

ADDITIONAL INFORMATION

Lorem ipsum dolor sit amet, consectetur adipiscing elit, sed do eiusmod tempor incididunt ut labore et dolore magna aliqua. Ut enim ad minim veniam, quis nostrud exercitation ullamco laboris nisi ut aliquip ex ea commodo consequat.

Summary of qualifications

Highly qualified and detail-oriented professional. Have excellent communication skills, demonstrated by over 10 years of experience in costumer relations and team collaborations. Have the abilities to adapt into different environments rapidly. Forward thinking with identifying problems and giving efficient solutions.

Experience

2012- 2017: Consulate General of Israel , Los Angeles, California

Consular Department: assisting Israeli citizens to obtain passport / documentations from Israeli officials. Examining and providing visas and other various services, to non- citizens who wish to work/ study/ travel to Israel. Accompany and supporting the clients throughout the wholes process and maintain professional customer relations.

2008-2012: El-Al Israeli Airlines , Tel Aviv Israel

Flight attendant: customer service at the business department. Working in different aircrafts, with various teams. Providing services and safety in a limited time-frame and different environments.

2006-2007: Electra Real Estate, Tel Aviv, Israel

CEO Secretary: Administrative operations and managing the CEO department at one of the leading real estate companies in Israel. That traded at the Tel Aviv Stock- Exchange.

2004-2006: David Intercontinental Hotel, Tel Aviv , Israel

Guest Relations Department: responsible for VIP guest service. Planning VIP events as well as VIP customer retention and distribution of the hotel chain membership.

2004: Impact Company Tel Aviv, Israel

Ground Hostess / PR representative : Hosting special events, conventions and exhibitions.

2001-2004: Israeli Defense Force, Tel Aviv, Israel

Officer: at the Communication and Computer Forces. Served at a secret electronic-warfare unit. Military rank: First Lieutenant.

Skills

Independent, Organized, representative, very responsible dedicated and loyal. As well as creative and initiative minded.

EXHIBIT #18

Applicant's Employment Verification Letters

iMpact
השפעה אורגנית

9/4/18

To whom it may concern,

Subject: Letter of employment for [redacted]

Dear Sir/Madam,

This letter is to certify that [redacted] worked at "Impact Company" as a Marketing and PR representative, between the dates: February/2004 - January/2005, April-July/2006 .

Sincerely,

Michal Shalem

CEO

IMPACT

אימפקט דיילות
ע.מ. 031946692

Scanned by CamScanner

INTERCONTINENTAL®
DAVID TEL AVIV

01 April 2018

To whom it may concern,

RE: *Employment's Permission*

We certify that [redacted] was employed at the David InterContinental Hotel Tel-Aviv, in the position of Guest Ralaition Representative from December 2004 until March 2006.

Best Regards,

Hila Amini
Asst. Director of Human Resources

David Inter-Continental Tel Aviv for and on behalf of Classic Hotel Management Limited
Kaufman St., P.O.Box 50155, Tel Aviv 61501 Israel Tel: (972-3)795 1111 Fax: (972-3) 795 1112 12
Internet site: www.intercontinental.com/telaviv e-mail: telaviv@interconti.com

CONSULATE GENERAL OF ISRAEL
LOS ANGELES

הקונסוליה הכללית של ישראל
לוס אנג'לס

August 24, 2017

To Whom It May Concern,

Re:

This is to confirm that was employed by the Consulate General of Israel in Los Angeles as Consular assistant from May 1st 2012 until April 28th 2017.

Sincerely,

Dalya Mizrahi
Consul

11766 Wilshire Boulevard, Suite 1600 Los Angeles, California 90025
Tel: (323) 852- 5500 Fax: (323) 852- 5551 embassies.gov.il/la

www.ingramcontent.com/pod-product-compliance
Lightning Source LLC
Chambersburg PA
CBHW061356240926
51846CB00007B/1428
* 9 7 8 1 9 4 8 7 7 4 8 2 6 *